THE MINOR KEYS

PLAYS BY DAVID BELKE
Swordplay: The Legend of the Princess Outlaw (1990)
The Maltese Bodkin (1991)
The Reluctant Resurrection of Sherlock Holmes (1992)
Blackpool and Parrish (1993)
April in Peril with Paul Morgan Donald (1994)
Another Two Hander or Two (1995)
The Crimson Yak with Paul Morgan Donald (1996)
The Red King's Dream (1996)
William the Bard (1997)
Riders of the Apocalypse: the reunion tour (1997)
Dreamland Saturday Nights (1998)
That Darn Plot (1998)
The Minor Keys (1999)
Ten Times Two (1999)
Win My Stuff with Cathleen Rootsaert (1999)
The Bonus Cigarettes Program (2000)

THE MINOR KEYS
A Romantic Comedy

David Belke

 Prairie Play Series: 18/Series Editor, Diane Bessai

© Copyright David Belke 2000
All rights reserved. The use of any part of this publication reproduced, transmitted in any form or by any means, electronic, mechanical, recording or otherwise, or stored in a retrieval system, without the prior consent of the publisher is an infringement of the copyright law. In the case of photocopying or other reprographic copying of the material, a licence must be obtained from the Canadian Reprography Collective before proceeding.

Production Rights: Rights to amateur productions of this play may be obtained through Playwrights' Union of Canada, 54 Wolseley St., 2nd Fl. Toronto, Ontario, Canada, M5T 1A5. Rights to any other productions, theatrical or otherwise, may be obtained through the playwright in care of Shadow Theatre, 10329 83 Ave. Edmonton, Alberta, Canada, T6E 2C6.

Canadian Cataloguing in Publication Data
Belke, David.
    The minor keys

(Prairie play series ; 18)
ISBN 1-896300-19-7

I. Title. II. Series.
PS8553.E4554M56 2000   C812'.54   C00-910229-9
PR9199.3.B3772M56 2000

Editor for the Press: Anne Nothof
Interior image: Trevor Schmidt
Cover design: Bob Young
Cover photograph: Darren Greenwood Photography *(Paul Morgan Donald as Hank Jeeter and Kerry Ann Doherty as Tracy Mason, Shadow Theatre, April 1999)*
Author photograph by Greg Southan reprinted with the permission of the *Edmonton Journal*

NeWest Press acknowledges the support of the Canada Council for the Arts for our publishing program. We also acknowledge the financial support of the Government of Canada through the Book Publishing Industry Development Program (BPIDP) for our publishing activities.

Acknowledgements: To the Pleasure Island Jazz Company, which inspired the play. To The Alberta Foundation for the Arts, who supported the play. To the New Varscona Theatre, who hosted the play. To Anne Nothof and NeWest Press, who published the play. And to Shadow Theatre, who provided the play with life, especially John Hudson, Coralie Cairns, John Sproule and the talented (and oh so patient) company of the first production.

NeWest Publishers Limited
Suite 201, 8540-109 Street
Edmonton, Alberta T6G 1E6
(780) 432-9427

To Bobbie and Ted, a.k.a. Mom and Dad,
for patient support and encouragement.
They trusted that I just might know what I was doing.

CONTENTS

INTRODUCTION	ix

THE MINOR KEYS	1

INTRODUCTION

There is this scene in *Night and Day,* the film biography of Cole Porter. Cole (played improbably by Cary Grant) is seated at a piano experimenting with a melody. He looks up from the keyboard to see a grandfather clock. "Like the tick tick tock of the stately clock, as it stands against the wall," mutters Cary/Cole. Then his attention is caught by the sound of raindrops on a nearby windowpane, causing him to remark, "Like the drip, drip, drip of the raindrops when the summer shower is through." And before you know it, he's writing *Night and Day.*

Inspiration is rarely that simple. Certainly there are those singular moments when an idea suddenly bursts into being, but if inspiration is a spark it needs kindling to start a fire. So it was with *The Minor Keys,* a play born of one part inspiration and many parts forethought and afterthought.

In the mid-90s, my continuing self-education as a playwright led me to explore new ground. Previously my plays had been rather big, sometimes even apocalyptic in scale, but now I was looking at the other end of the scale. I started exploring small characters with modest dreams and quiet ambitions.

The Red King's Dream (1996) was the first step in this direction and it was the first play that I poured my own personal experiences into. The play followed a solitary, socially awkward individual as he stumbled into love. It wasn't a big story. It wasn't earth-shattering. It was bittersweet: a comedy with a tinge of tragedy. But it was personally very satisfying, and incidentally, a huge hit.

A year later I wrote *Dreamland Saturday Nights,* another small-scale play, whose central character was a woman absorbed in the fantasy world of the movies, but who discovered romance and the ability to stand up for herself. Once again the play was personally satisfying, a theatrical hit, a critical success, and it won a Sterling Award as the Outstanding New Play of the Year.

Encouraged by my successful forays into the world of minor-key characters, I started thinking about what would be the next development. I had written about a modest, understated man, and followed it with a play about a modest, understated woman. Where to go next?

What about a modest, understated cast? Combining characters of small dreams and quiet ambitions just might add up to a play greater than the sum of its parts. Intriguing. But what kind of characters? What would link them together? A setting perhaps? Or maybe a mood? How do you find structure for such a play? As is my habit, I filed the idea away in the back of my mind to let it percolate for a while. And so it was with that notion merrily bubbling away in my unconscious that I went to Walt Disney World.

Well, not Disney World really. My compatriots from Shadow Theatre and I were on our way to the Orlando Fringe Festival to present one of my plays, *Another Two Hander or Two*. Playing the male lead was Shadow's artistic director John Hudson, and also along for the ride and sunshine were actors and Shadow stalwarts Coralie Cairns and John Sproule. Along with myself, this gang of four forms the artistic nucleus of Shadow Theatre.

Shadow Theatre, the company which graciously produces my plays and theoretically employs me as resident playwright, resident designer and producer, was born of the Edmonton Fringe in 1990. It has grown into a lively producing organization that presents an annual four-show subscription season at the New Varscona Theatre. The growth of the company has been overseen by John, John, Coralie and myself, with the help of an outstanding board and a wealth of talented theatre artists. In the theatre-mad city of Edmonton, Shadow Theatre is still pretty small scale financially, but artistically it is competing with distinction in the big leagues. There are still some days when the staff has to forego salaries in order to keep the company afloat, but there is something thrilling and addictive about working with such talented and committed theatre artists. The New Varscona Theatre is one of busiest theatre facilities in the country. It is home to companies such as Shadow, Teatro la Quindicina, Die-Nasty and many others. Varscona artists not only produce in the space, but also manage and care for the facility. (I think it is a circumstance unique in Canada.)

Back to Florida.

The Orlando Fringe can be a great deal of fun. The people there are helpful, supportive and friendly. The festival is modest, but produces some excellent work, and also draws the attention of American producers, meaning there can be further production opportunities. And besides, there is something very appealing about doing rehearsals in the tropic sun.

And then there are the theme parks.

Whenever we had a free day, the siren call of the theme parks beckoned our little Canadian tourist hearts. One day we had a noon show at the Orlando Fringe (small audience, hot venue), so that meant we had the evening off. And one of our actors, Amy Berger (the future leading lady of *Dreamland Saturday Nights*), knew exactly where she wanted us to spend our free night: Pleasure Island.

Give them credit, those Disney people are smart. Since all the theme parks in Disney World close around 10:00 P.M., they realized they had thousands of vacationing tourist adults who needed something to do. And so Pleasure Island was created: a collection of nightclubs built to appeal to a variety of tastes and dispositions, and all open past midnight.

It was a bewilderingly appealing tangle of buildings and attractions that greeted us when we arrived at Disney's answer to adult entertainment, but it was the supper hour and the first order of business was to find some place to eat. Many of the clubs were already crowded, but at the far end of the island, tucked in by an arcade, we found a pleasantly modest looking building that served dinner. It was a jazz club.

The atmosphere was attractive. The music was smooth and calming. The lighting was dim. The knots in my muscles began to loosen. Scanning the club, I could see a wide variety of different people: musicians lost in their music as only jazz musicians could be; staff floating amidst the tables delivering drinks and meals and then fading into the background; patrons, some absorbed in the music, some conversing as the soft saxophone tones provided aural wallpaper. One was even reading. What a great collection of characters. What wonderful atmosphere. And since jazz has never been a truly mainstream music form, it would suit a cast of modest characters with small dreams and quiet ambitions. Somebody should write a play—

Spark!

Minor key music for minor key people!

Soon I was scribbling down ideas, characters, impressions, and plot points on a Pleasure Island doodle pad. Almost all the characters in *The Minor Keys* were born in that moment. Jazz provided the inspiration, and it also provided me with the structure I was looking for.

Every instrument in a jazz combo gets its opportunity to contribute to the whole. One instrument will take the lead for a while, then slide back to support another instrument's lead. The characters of my play would be like jazz instruments. Each character would have his or her own story, but would also be supporting characters in other stories. And like a cool jazz composition, there would be no breaks in the play either. Scenes would smoothly crossfade, sometimes helped by a character moving from one location to another, sometimes by a remark, sometimes because a character simply demanded attention. And throughout the entire play there would be music. Sometimes it would be in the background; sometimes a song would be performed live. Jazz rhythms would shape the play.

Cool.

After I had filled a couple of pages of the pad, the inspirational moment passed. My friends and I finished our dinners and spent a pleasant evening in the land of the Mouse. However, my dinner companions who were witnesses to my epiphany would not soon forget it. Especially not John Hudson.

And so in early 1998, the artistic director of Shadow Theatre and I were talking about possibilities for our ninth season. John remarked, "So what about that jazz play of yours? I think I'd like to see it."

So did I.

The Minor Keys was commissioned as part of Shadow's 1998-1999 season. Of the people who were present at the moment of inspiration, four ended up working on the play. John Hudson directed, happily Coralie Cairns and Amy Berger (two of my favorite actors) were cast as bartender and accountant respectively, and John Sproule came on board as dramaturge. Also invited to join the cast was the indispensable Paul Morgan Donald. Paul is not only one of the few performers in town who is also an accomplished musician, but Paul's talents as a composer, an arranger, and a writer with a keen sense of character and plot would be foundations upon which the play grew. Another accomplished musician/actor was Rick Ash, whose skill as a blues harmonica player also turned into a valuable resource, as were Kerry Ann Doherty's talents as a jazz vocalist. Rounding out the cast were comic actors Jacob Banigan and Andrew Mecready, who respectively brought conniving charm and a poetic soul into the mix. With the outstanding visual interpretations of designer Trevor Schmidt and stage manager Wayne Paquette to hold the whole thing together, the perfect company to bring *The Minor Keys* to life was assembled.

Between conception and opening night there would be many rewrites and revisions to help this play achieve its potential. A lot of hard work and deep thought went into this play. Sometimes nerves would fray. But eventually we got there. And all through the difficulties, one thing kept everyone on track. That moment of inspiration when everything became clear guided me through the entire process and served as a connection for everyone who was there to witness it. And it brought us to this publication.

Songs and plays do not appear completely out of thin air. But trust me, inspiration can happen. And when the spark ignites, you had better be ready with kindling and a notepad.

—David Belke
Ardrossan Alberta, February 2000

The Minor Keys was first produced by Shadow Theatre at the New Varscona Theatre in Edmonton, Alberta, April 3-18, under the direction of John Hudson.

CAST

Professor Ron Damon — *Andrew Mecready*
Mickey MacDuff/Buddy Quirrely — *Jacob Banigan*
Amelia Blue — *Coralie Cairns*
Tracy Mason/Foley — *Kerry Ann Doherty*
Moonlight Baker/"Little Mike" Conroy — *Rick Ash*
Hank Jeeter — *Paul Morgan Donald*
Edie Moss — *Amy Berger*

Paul Morgan Donald — *Musical Director*
Wayne Paquette — *Stage Manager*
Trevor Schmidt — *Set & Costume Design*
David Belke — *Lighting Design*
John Sproule — *Dramaturge*

THE MINOR KEYS

THE CHARACTERS IN ORDER OF APPEARANCE

Professor Ron Damon, professor of English literature, regular patron of the Combo Club, fifties

Mickey MacDuff, bass player, Hank Jeeter's sideman, mid twenties

Amelia Blue, Combo Club bartender, thirties

Tracy Mason, potential vocalist, MacDuff's girlfriend, early thirties

Moonlight Baker, the club's caretaker and handyman, fifties

Hank Jeeter, long time jazz guitarist, currently owner and manager of the Combo Club, the star attraction, late thirties

Edie Moss, accountant, early twenties

Buddy Quirrely, the bebop Buddhist, potential buyer of the Combo Club (played by the same actor as MacDuff)

Little Mike Conroy, loan shark, a dangerous man to borrow money from (played by the same actor as Moonlight)

Foley, the piano player (played by the same actor as Tracy)

THE SETTING

The Combo Club, April 1963. Act One: P.M., Act Two: A.M.

PRODUCTION NOTES

This play is designed to simulate the rhythms and textures of a jazz composition. If you think of the characters as instruments, then as in jazz one instrument will take the lead for a moment before slipping into a secondary role as another instrument begins to improvise a melody. There should be no blackouts within the acts. Each scene should flow and blend into the other. In other words, lots of crossfades. Actors remain on-stage in the black, to be picked up by the lights later when their scene comes up.

Also, like any good jazz group, this cast of characters is essentially lacking a lead. All the instruments (characters) take the primary lead at different points in the action, and every character is the supporting character in another character's story. For example, Edie's story is essentially one of gaining confidence and independence, but she is also an aggravation to Hank, a love interest for MacDuff, and an advisor to Amelia and Damon.

In the original production, Hank played guitar, although almost any jazz instrument would be appropriate for his part. Moonlight plays harmonica (being an instrument that he can easily carry around in his pocket). Tracy must be a credible singer, but on the other hand, MacDuff does not actually have to play bass, nor does Foley have to play piano.

ACT ONE
P.M.

April, 1963. The place is the Combo Club, a rundown but pleasantly atmospheric jazz club on a not-so-popular side of town of a medium-sized American city. The building the club inhabits is a little dilapidated, but for a real jazz fan the Combo Club is hard to beat. Scenes take place in a variety of locations through the building, and each location can be isolated to give focus.

From right to left the locations are the house, where the club audience resides. It has two tables with chairs, as well as some booths in shadowy corners. Occupying a place of importance is the bar where as many as three people can sit comfortably. Behind the bar hangs a well-worn sign proudly identifying the location as "The Combo Cl b." Where the "u" has gone is anybody's guess.

Left of the bar is the green room, a place behind the stage where the performers relax between sets. It has a faded couch and some over-used chairs along with other scavenged furniture pieces. There is also a dressing table and phone. The green room has an open entrance to the stage, but we never actually see the performances until Act Two when the green room transforms into the stage.

Left of the green room there is an alley in back of the club. Shadowy and rundown, it nonetheless is a safe place to escape the atmosphere of the club. A door opens to the inside.

For the top of show we are in a twilit land of nowhere. A bass beat rhythm plays underneath. A light picks out Professor Damon.

Damon: What is jazz?

A light finds MacDuff.

MacDuff: It's music right? But it's more than that. It stands for something.

Damon: Something obscure.

MacDuff: It's about . . . love and danger—

Damon: Sex and drink—

MacDuff: Chicks and smokes. What is jazz?

Damon: Jazz has its roots in ragtime which saw its apotheosis in the southern United States. To search for the development of the jazz music style—

MacDuff: Jazz is cool.

Damon: One need only look at such pioneers as Jelly Roll Morton—

MacDuff: You can't have one without the other.

Damon: Bix Beiderbecke—

MacDuff: So what is cool? *Thinks.*

Damon: Fats Waller, Louis Armstrong among other seminal influences.

MacDuff: Cool is cool.

Damon *in unison*	**MacDuff** *in unison*
Now Morton's contribution led to an opening up of harmonies which led in the creation of larger bands and also numerous solo artists.	I guess it's more of feeling. A feeling of freedom. You can do your own stuff. You can't always do your own stuff. Not always.

MacDuff & Damon: So what is jazz?

Lights up on Amelia delivering a box of booze to the bar.

Amelia: I don't have time for this.

Damon: America's only native art form.

Amelia: I have to set up the bar—

MacDuff: It's music for hustlers.

Amelia: Unpack supplies.

MacDuff: So what is jazz?

Damon: The 30s are the era I like to refer to as the Golden Age of swing. You would likely recognize the luminaries of that period . . .

Light up on Tracy.

Tracy: What is jazz?

Damon: Benny Goodman, Count Basie, Duke Ellington . . .

Amelia: Oh, I love Duke Ellington.

Tracy: I listen to it all the time.

Amelia: I also like Miles Davis.

MacDuff: Jazz is an attitude, not a melody.

Amelia: And I love Ella Fitzgerald.

Tracy: I'll listen to records all through the night. Letting it all soak in.

Amelia: *Unpacking bottles.* I don't have time for this.

Tracy: I carry the music in my head.

Amelia: We have to open . . .

MacDuff: Jazz is a state of mind.

Tracy: Jazz is like a blanket. It wraps itself around you.

Damon: There are many different kinds of jazz.

MacDuff: You can find your own way.

Damon: There is bebop, rebop, cubop and hard bop—

Tracy: Sometimes I sing.

Damon: Free, cool, progressive and swing.

MacDuff: You've got to feel your way through the music.

Tracy: When I'm alone—

Amelia: Jazz is an opinion.

Tracy: And can't help myself.

Damon: Modalism, formalism, third stream and scat—

Tracy: It just comes out.

All: So what is jazz?

Light up on Moonlight.

Moonlight: I'll tell you what jazz is.

Damon: Jazz is an intellectual exercise.

Amelia: That's a horrible thing to say.

Moonlight: It's more than just a label. It's a way of thinking, a way of being, a way of showing who you are.

Damon: What is jazz?

Moonlight: If you gotta ask the question, then you'll never know the answer.

The dialogue overlaps.

MacDuff: Jazz is the performer.

    Damon: Jazz is the structure.

        Amelia: Jazz is the atmosphere.

            Moonlight: Jazz is the compulsion.

                Tracy: Jazz is the sensation.

MacDuff: Jazz is the band.

    Amelia: Jazz is the life.

        Tracy: Jazz is the sound.

            Damon: Jazz is the form.

Pause. The cast breathes a sigh.

Moonlight: Jazz is the heart.

Moonlight plays a jazzy blues riff on the harmonica. Hank wanders in, guitar in hand.

Hank: You want to know what jazz is? It's played on the black rather than the white keys. It's minor key music for minor key people.

Hank exits. MacDuff, Damon, and Tracy disperse. Moonlight continues playing.

MacDuff: Bitter man.

Damon: Vitriolic.

Tracy: What is he talking about?

MacDuff: He's lost the spark.

Alone, Amelia addresses the audience.

Amelia: The minor keys. The people who don't make a difference. The people whose struggles are known only to themselves. They live on the minor keys. And that . . . well, that is jazz.

The lights and the harmonica fade. Music continues to seep out from the club, although muffled now as heard from the alley.

Edie Moss stumbles into the alley. In her twenties and dressed in a conservative fashion, she is a rather attractive woman, although she does tend to keep her light under a bushel. She moves quickly, keeping one eye on her surroundings and the other on the scrap of paper with an address. She is burdened with a briefcase, a pile of loose papers, and an electric adding machine slung under one arm. The cord from the adding machine dangles dangerously close to Edie's feet.

Inevitably she stumbles. Although she manages to save the fragile adding machine, the briefcase and all the papers spill out onto the ground. Edie sits defeated in the mess. She starts gathering her things and then pauses. For the first time she really listens to the music filtering into the alley. She soaks in the melody. She is so absorbed that she doesn't hear the approach of another person into the alley. He is distinguished and in late middle age, and he too carries a briefcase. This is Professor Ron Damon.

Damon: Good isn't it? *Edie is startled. She grabs as many of her things as possible and backs into a corner.* So sorry. I heard the commotion in the alley. Never know when another hand might be needed for a knife fight. Are you in need of some assistance?

Edie: Some. I guess. I'm sorry. I dropped . . .

Damon: *Helping to gather things up.* I see.

Edie: And I'm late. I was looking for this address and I got turned around. And I couldn't find a parking space. And I'm late . . .

Damon: *Scrutinizing a paper.* Are you some sort of bookkeeper?

Edie: How did you . . . ?

Damon: If I am not mistaken, these are accounting sheets.

Edie: Oh. Yes. They are. I am. An accountant. A CPA.

Damon: Rather young for an accountant aren't you?

Edie: *Sharply.* Old enough to add. *Then relaxing.* Sorry. It's just I get that a lot. I'm not making the best impression am I?

Damon: Nonsense. Perfectly charming. In a disjointed sort of way. I don't believe we've been formally introduced.

Edie: Edith Moss. CPA. My friends call me Edie.

Damon: Then I shall endeavour to call you Edie. Ron Damon. Hello.

Edie: I've got a card here somewhere. I'm sure I do. Just give me a sec. If you ever need anyone to do your taxes. . . . Here we are. *Edie produces a rumpled card from her pocket. Damon accepts it.*

Damon: Thank you. I shall treasure it.

Pause. They have finished gathering together Edie's things. The two listen to the music for a moment.

Damon: Sometimes I just stand outside this building and listen to the muffled music seep through the walls. Beautiful isn't it?

Edie: I guess. I don't know. I'm not an expert or anything.

Damon: You were looking for an address?

Edie: I was following the music.

Damon: You must be on your way to the Combo Club.

Edie: Now how did . . . ? I know that isn't written on the balance sheets.

Damon: Elementary my dear, Watson. Firstly, if you were following the music it seems unlikely that you would be on your way to the warehouse across the alley. Secondly, the Combo Club is one of the few places in this area open on a Saturday night. And thirdly, since you are in fact standing by the back door of the establishment, it seems likely the Combo Club is your destination.

Edie: You're a detective.

Damon: Worse. I'm a professor of English literature.

Edie: No kidding.

Damon: None at all.

Edie: Sounds fascinating.

Damon: About as fascinating as an Archie comic.

Edie: That bad?

Damon: Yes.

Edie: Sorry.

Damon: It's destiny that owes me the apology. So shall I play Virgil to your Allegheri?

Edie: I have no idea what you are talking about.

Damon: No need to fear. As the night wears on and I become more inebriate, I develop my own annotations.

Before he can open the door, it is opened by Moonlight taking out the garbage.

Moonlight: Evening, Professor.

Damon: Good evening, Moonlight.

Moonlight: Got a date tonight?

Damon: Merely a wayward actuary in search of sanctuary.

Moonlight: I have no idea what you are talking about.

Damon: Edith Moss meet Moonlight Baker.

Moonlight: *Indicating the garbage.* I'll understand if you don't want to shake hands.

Damon: How's the show tonight?

Moonlight: Hank's fingering is off again. It's like he has his mind on something else. MacDuff keeps trying to keep things moving, but there's not much a sideman can do if the lead ain't taking the lead. And Foley? Foley's in her own little world on the keys.

Damon: Moonlight fancies himself a bit of a jazz expert.

Edie: Are you a musician?

Moonlight: I just clean up around here, Miss.

Damon: So, not very good tonight?

Moonlight: Hank has just been dragging these last few months. I don't get it.

Edie: I think it sounds nice.

Damon: If you think it sounds good out here, then wait until you hear it inside.

Moonlight: By the way, have you heard the word?

Damon: Words are my livelihood. I'm always willing to add another to the lexicon.

Moonlight: Buddy Quirrely is in town.

Damon: The bebop Buddhist?

Moonlight: Still questing for the Great Soul.

Damon: I thought he was in Europe.

Moonlight: Friend of a friend saw him check into the Hilton round noon.

Damon: Hardly reliable information.

Moonlight: Maybe he'll come here. Wouldn't that be something?

Edie: Who's Buddy Quirrely? A legend?

Moonlight: A rumour.

Damon: A nut. Thank you for your insights, Mr. Baker.

Moonlight: Always happy to educate the educated. Pleasure, Miss. *Exits.*

Damon: Come Alice. The rabbit hole awaits.

Damon offers his arm to Edie and he leads her through the back door of the Combo Club. There is the muted buzz of voices, but what fills the air is the music. Edie is a little overwhelmed by it all, but Damon is completely at home.

Damon: Welcome, my dear Edie, to Shangri-La, to the land of the lotus eaters, and a little bit of southside Chicago in the night. In short, welcome to the Combo Club, my revivifier, relaxant and retreat from the weary world.

Edie: Most people would simply say, "We're here."

Damon: Excess verbiage is a virtue in the ivy-covered halls of academe. I shall try to exercise my vocabulary in a more concise fashion. *Adopting a flat accent.* Come on, Edie, let's ankle.

Edie: I'm supposed to see the owner.

Damon: You see that man on stage? The one with the guitar? That is the one and only Hank Jeeter. Pater familias, *éminence grise* and owner of the Combo Club.

Edie: He is?

Damon: And I don't think he'll appreciate you interrupting his set in order to discuss finances.

Edie: So what do I do?

Damon: He shall soon be on break. In the interim, let us hie ourselves to the vendor of libations.

Damon and Edie arrive at the bar. Damon puts his briefcase down on top. Edie holds onto her belongings.

Damon: That's odd.

Edie: What?

Damon: I don't see Amelia anywhere. She is usually either behind the bar or serving. She is the one person who keeps this club from falling apart.

Edie: I thought Mr. Jeeter was the owner.

Damon: Mr. Jeeter may pay the bills, but Amelia is better than an owner. She is a bartender. More than a bartender, the Platonic ideal of bartenders.

Edie: And that's good?

Damon: A nonpareil. A paragon. The most stellar of stewards.

Edie: You must really like her.

Damon: That I do. *Pause.* Can you keep a secret? Then let me show you something. *He produces a little box containing an engagement ring.*

Edie: Oh, it's beautiful.

Damon: As is its recipient. I must admit a certain tremulousness. Tonight, after years basking in her glow, I am proposing a far more immutable relationship.

Edie: You're in love.

Damon: I never found the company of another human being to be near as harmonious as the time I have spent with Amelia Blue.

Edie: Good luck. *Passing back the box.*

Damon: Luck has nothing to do with it. It is simply a matter of finding the perfect moment to act. Ah, there she is.

Enter Amelia Blue with monkey wrench. An attractive thirty-five- year-old, she is comfortable in her job and the place she has found herself. However at this precise moment, the club's faulty plumbing has upset her usual equilibrium.

Amelia: This place is a dump.

Damon: *To Edie.* I told you she was beautiful.

Amelia: Hey, Professor. You're late.

Damon: I was the victim of another ridiculously long faculty meeting. But I am most disappointed in you, my sweet "Dulcinea."

Amelia: Cyrano de Bergerac?

Damon: Don Quixote. Imagine my horror when I found that you had abandoned your post. As one of the constant stars in my universe, I expect you to remain firmly fixed.

Amelia: Had to turn off the water in the men's room. One of the sinks was overflowing. This place is falling apart.

Damon: I prefer to think of it as aesthetically decayed.

Amelia: Well, you're a romantic. *To Edie.* Can I help you?

Edie: Soda, please.

Damon: *As Amelia fixes Edie's drink.* And you are the realist who keeps me grounded, my dear Roxanne.

Amelia: Don Quixote?

Damon: Cyrano de Bergerac. It would aid your memory if you actually read the books.

Amelia: When? I soak up what you share. I enjoy being a sponge.

Damon: I'll raise you out of the invertebrates yet.

Amelia: Better men than you have tried.

Damon: Touché.

Amelia: Are you ready to order?

Damon: Yes, indeed. It's going to be a long, dark night of the soul. *Taking essays out of his briefcase.*

Amelia: And what are we marking tonight?

Damon: Second year essays on romantic poetry appropriately enough.

Amelia: Why appropriate?

Damon: *Winks at Edie.* Tonight it shall be scotch. Bring the bottle, a tumbler and your sympathy.

Amelia: That bad?

Damon: Fifty-eight half-asleep students who think a sonnet is something you wear in the Easter parade.

Amelia: *Delivering the bottle and glass.* If I can learn, they can learn.

Damon: You're different, my darling. When I talk about Tennyson, you actually pretend to listen.

Amelia: I get paid to pretend to listen.

Damon: And you do it so charmingly, my darling Hebe.

Amelia: Thank you.

Edie: I thought your name was Amelia?

Damon: An affectionate nickname. Hebe was the cup bearer to the Greek gods.

Amelia: She was the Olympian bartender.

Damon: *Indicating Amelia.* My best pupil.

Amelia: *Indicating Edie.* Friend of yours?

Damon: Edith and/or Edie Moss, meet Amelia the bartender. Amelia is the Persephone at the heart of our jazz-based underworld.

Amelia: Amelia Blue, actually. Amelia the bartender is just my stage name.

Edie: Hello.

Damon: She's here to see Hank.

Amelia: Fan?

Edie: Business.

Damon: Miss Moss is an accountant.

Amelia: An accountant? He didn't mention anything about this to me.

Damon: Maybe there's a problem with the books.

Amelia: Probably overreacting.

Damon: He's been doing a lot of that lately.

Amelia: Ever since I wrote that cheque.

Damon: And which cheque would that be?

Amelia: Two weeks ago, I noticed that the windows in the alley were broken. It's about two hundred dollars to get them fixed and I knew we had money in the bank, so I wrote the cheque.

Damon: Perfectly reasonable.

Amelia: That's what I thought. But Hank goes through the roof. The next thing I know he's splitting up all the duties into his department and my department.

Edie: Actually a clear division of management responsibilities is a sound business practice. With a clear structure of duties then there is never any confusion and less overlap of . . . *Seeing Amelia's cold stare.* But then again it's always nice to know what is going on.

Amelia: Ever since the windows he's cut back on my duties. He's doing all the little jobs I used to do.

Edie: Oh dear.

Damon: What is it?

Edie: This all sounds very familiar.

Amelia: What do you mean?

Edie: Upset employer. Reduction of duties. Lack of consultation. Those are the signs.

Amelia: Signs of what?

Edie: I shouldn't be saying anything. It's just . . . Do you have any kind of job security?

Amelia: Job security?

Edie: It sounds to me like he might be preparing to . . . I'm probably wrong. But if you have an unhappy employer who is cutting back on your duties . . .

Amelia: Oh my God! He's going to fire me?

Damon: This is nonsense. Hebe is an essential part of this establishment.

Amelia: He was really upset about the cheque.

Edie: I could be wrong.

Damon: Over one cheque?

Edie: People have been fired for less. I'm sorry . . .

Damon: There must be something that can be done.

Edie: Prove you're indispensable.

Amelia: I *am* indispensable.

Edie: Let him see you at work. Take the initiative. Show enthusiasm.

A stranger passes the bar. He is a nondescript man dressed in something suggesting an Asian aesthetic, although he also wears sunglasses and a blue beret. He pauses, absorbing the atmosphere. We will later learn this is Buddy Quirrely.

Amelia: *Noticing Buddy, then quickly.* Can I help you?

Buddy: Just looking.

Amelia: Maybe I can help you look.

Buddy: I'm looking for the Bird.

Damon: The Bird?

Edie: Maybe he means the washroom.

Buddy: Have you got the Bird, pilgrim?

Damon: That sounded vaguely indecent.

Amelia: No birds here. Is there anything else I can help you with?

Buddy: I'll just keep looking.

Amelia: Just don't disturb the other customers.

Buddy: One can only disturb the surface of an ocean, the depths remain ever calm. *Exits.*

Edie: Who was that?

Amelia: Damned if I know.

Edie: Seems a little odd.

Damon: "We're all mad here. I'm mad. You're mad."

Edie: Excuse me?

Amelia: "Alice in Wonderland."

Damon: Just a little quotation by way of illustration.

The music finishes. There is some applause.

Edie: I have to go. I wish I could stay, but you know . . .

Damon: "You're late. You're late."

Edie: Couldn't find a parking space.

Amelia: Green room. Back to your right. Can't miss it.

Damon: If you want to visit, I'll be here all night. Conscious or un, depending on the quality of the scotch or the lack thereof in my students' dissertations.

Edie: Good luck. *Beat.* With everything. *Exits.*

Damon: Now that we are alone, there is something I wish to ask you—

Amelia: Fire me?!

Tracy Mason tentatively approaches the bar.

Tracy: Excuse me?

Amelia: Can I help you?

Tracy: Yes. Hello. I'm looking for MacDuff? Mickey MacDuff? He's a musician here.

Amelia: He's usually backstage between sets.

Tracy: Oh. Good.

Amelia: They don't like visitors backstage. I'd be happy to get a message to him.

Tracy: No. That's all right. He's expecting, was expecting me. I'm late.

Amelia: Couldn't find a parking space?

Tracy: I walked. Was walking. I was walking around the block. I just . . . Where did you say he was?

Amelia: In the green room.

Tracy: Green room?

Amelia: Back to the right. Can't miss it.

Tracy: Thank you. Thank you very much. *Heads to the green room.*

Amelia: Sorry, Professor. You were going to ask me something?

Damon: *By way of proposal.*
"Come live with me, and be my love;
And we will all the pleasures prove—"

Amelia: Oh. I love that one. *Exits with drinks.*

Edie enters the green room. Mickey MacDuff is there. An energetic and impulsive young man, he also plays bass as Hank's sideman.

Edie: Is this where I'll find Mr. Jeeter?

MacDuff: He had some business to take care of.

Edie: I was told he'd be here.

MacDuff: He left his guitar. He'll have to come back for that. I don't think we've been introduced. I'm—

Tracy enters the green room with a shy knock.

MacDuff: Tracy. There you are. You were supposed to be here at the beginning of the evening.

Tracy: I know. I got nervous. I almost didn't come.

MacDuff: I've been telling Hank all about you, Babe.

Tracy: He really wants to hear me?

MacDuff: Of course he does.

Tracy: Hank Jeeter? I'm so nervous.

MacDuff: You have nothing to be nervous about.

Tracy: But he's a real musician. A real professional jazz musician.

MacDuff: So am I.

Tracy: But he has records and everything. He's worked with so many people.

MacDuff: So have I.

Tracy: I'm no singer. I should go—

MacDuff: Oh come on. Didn't I tell you you were terrific. Right from the moment I first heard you?

Tracy: Yes.

MacDuff: So all you have to do is show Jeeter the same thing you showed me.

Tracy: It's different.

MacDuff: How is it different?

Tracy: I can't sing with people watching. It's too . . . embarrassing.

MacDuff: Don't you trust me?

Tracy: Of course I do. It's just . . .

MacDuff: Good. Then it's settled.

Tracy: I wish I had my records.

MacDuff: Don't get all twisted up about this. Just let it all come out like you did this morning and you'll be fine.

Tracy: I'll be fine?

MacDuff: You'll be more than fine. Now all we need is Hank Jeeter.

Focus shifts to the bar. As Hank talks on the phone, Damon watches out of the corner of his eye.

Hank: No. I ordered one thousand cocktail napkins. Not dinner napkins, cocktail napkins. I can't use them. I'm not going to pay for something I can't use.

Amelia arrives having just served drinks.

Hank: No, I can't use them. They're too big. That's why. Dinner napkins are bigger than cocktail napkins. You know that. Yes, I have scissors.

Amelia takes the phone away from Hank.

Amelia: Hello? It's me. We ordered cocktail napkins. Yes, *those* cocktail napkins. Good. Have them here on Monday. Thanks. Bye. *She hangs up and gives Hank a hard look.*

Hank: I saw the boxes in the kitchen. I could see they weren't right—

Amelia: Their mistake. I'll take care of it.

Hank: If you don't, I will.

Amelia: Don't you trust me?

Hank: I trusted you until you wrote that cheque.

Amelia: But the windows—

Hank: The only thing you should be spending money on is food and drink.

Amelia: I was just trying to do my job.

Hank: *Exiting.* Glad to hear it. Everything has to be perfect tonight.

Damon: Then I suppose you haven't heard about the men's room.

Amelia tries to shush Damon, but it is too late. Hank freezes.

Hank: The men's room?

Amelia: It's nothing.

Hank: What about the men's room?

Amelia: It's nothing. Nothing really.

Hank: What? What happened? *Amelia refuses to answer, so he turns his attention to Damon.* Well? What happened in the men's room?

ACT ONE 19

Damon: *Seeing Amelia's expression.* I have no idea what you're talking about.

Hank: *Back to Amelia.* You know, all I have to do is just walk in there.

Amelia: *Pause, then realizing it cannot be hidden any longer.* One of the faucets popped off.

Hank: Popped off? And?

Amelia: And I turned off the water.

Hank: You turned off the water?

Amelia: Yes.

Hank: In the men's room?

Amelia: It was either that or start planting rice in the stalls.

Hank: What if someone has to go?

Amelia: I've been sending them across the street to the gas station. I'll call a plumber first thing in the morning.

Hank: Do you know how much a plumber costs? I'll take care of it.

Amelia: No. I'll take care of it.

Hank: I need you out here, not under a sink. Besides, I've spent the last four years of my life keeping those pipes together with bubble gum and busted guitar strings.

Damon: Maybe that's the problem.

Hank: No one knows them as well as I do.

Amelia: And what are we supposed to do if you hurt your hands? You have two more sets coming up.

Hank: I can always hum. Anything else?

Amelia: No.

Damon: The fire escape was down in the alley.

Amelia shoots Damon a disapproving look.

Hank: I'll take care of it. Anything else?

Damon: Well . . . *Glancing at Amelia.* No.

Hank: Fine. Now while I'm getting the faucet fixed, I want you to keep your eyes open. I'm expecting some people tonight.

Amelia: Who?

Hank: I've got a bookkeeper coming in.

Amelia: In the green room.

Hank: Why didn't you tell me?

Damon: She just did.

Amelia: Strange time to be meeting with an accountant, Hank.

Hank: My department, remember? I'm numbers, you're napkins.

Amelia: Anyone else?

Hank: Buddy Quirrely.

Damon: The bebop Buddhist?

Hank: I'm supposed to be meeting him after the midnight set.

Amelia: Something we need to discuss?

Hank: Just keep your eyes open.

Damon: What's he look like?

Hank: He'll be wearing shades and a blue beret.

Damon and Amelia exchange glances.

Damon & Amelia: The bird guy.

Hank: What bird guy?

Amelia: There was a guy. He said he was looking for birds.

Hank, Damon & Amelia: *Realization.* "Bird."

Hank: Where is he?

Amelia: He's around here somewhere.

Hank: Find him.

Amelia: I'll get Moonlight to do a search of the building. What do we do once we find him?

Hank: Hold on to him. I'll get back as soon as I can.

Amelia: And where will you be?

Hank: I've got to meet the accountant. Then I'll work on the faucet. Just find Quirrely. *Exits.*

Amelia: Well, you were a lot of help.

Damon: He asked a question. I simply answered.

Amelia: Then do me a favour, Professor. Stay away from questions for the rest of the night, okay? *Exits with drink tray.*

Damon: This is not going as well as I hoped.

Hank strides to the green room. When he arrives, Tracy, MacDuff, and Edie are waiting.

Hank: So. What's the deal?

MacDuff: I found us a singer.

Hank: Not you. I want to see the accountant.

Edie: That'll be me.

MacDuff: This is Tracy Mason.

Hank: *To Edie.* You're the accountant?

MacDuff: I told you about her?

Edie: Edie Moss. Hello.

Tracy: Hello.

Hank: You can't be the accountant.

Edie: Why not?

Tracy: Maybe we should go.

Hank: I spoke to a man.

MacDuff: *To Tracy* Don't worry—

Edie: That would be my father.

MacDuff: He's very excited to meet you.

Hank: I need a professional.

Edie: And they sent me.

MacDuff: Trust me.

Hank: I need someone experienced.

Edie: I'm a CPA.

Hank: But you're a—

MacDuff: Hank.

Hank: MacDuff. I have business to take care of.

MacDuff: Hank, this is Tracy Mason. She wants to be our new singer.

Tracy: Actually, I just . . .

Hank: We don't need a singer.

MacDuff: Tracy isn't just any singer. She's the best thing since . . . Billie Holliday.

Tracy: I'm not that good.

Hank: She doesn't think she's that good, MacDuff.

MacDuff: Give her a chance to show you what she's got.

Tracy: MacDuff. Mr. Jeeter is busy. It was a pleasure meeting you, Mr. Jeeter. I love your music.

Hank: You do?

ACT ONE 23

Tracy: I have all your albums.

Hank: Both of them?

Tracy: I listen to them all the time. You're very . . . I'm sorry, you probably hear this all the time.

Hank: Strangely enough, I don't.

MacDuff: She's always playing your records, Hank. She's a real fan.

Hank: Is she? *Pause.* Okay. Show me what you've got.

MacDuff: Come on, Trace. You're up.

Tracy: I am?

MacDuff: You'll be fine. Just stay relaxed.

Tracy: I'll try.

MacDuff: Don't worry. You can do it as long as I'm here.

Tracy: Stay close.

Hank: What are you going to sing for me?

Tracy: You want me to sing for you?

Hank: You've got one minute.

Tracy: One minute?

Hank: MacDuff . . .

MacDuff: Tracy. Go ahead.

Tracy: I'd like to sing "Stardust."

Hank: "Stardust"? Tough song.

Tracy: It is? Would you rather . . .

Hank: No, no. Go ahead. Sing whatever you like. *He glances at his watch.*

Tracy starts to sing "Stardust." Badly. Hank and MacDuff exchange glances.

Hank: Okay. Thank you, Miss Mason.

Tracy: You're welcome.

Hank: The fact of the matter is we're not really looking for a singer right now.

Tracy: I see.

Hank: Look. I appreciate your coming here. Maybe it would be better if we did this some other time.

Tracy: No, no, no. I don't want to bother you, Mr. Jeeter. I know your time is valuable.

Hank: Listen. If a job comes up, I will keep you in mind. It's just right now . . . Keep practicing.

Tracy: Thank you. I appreciate—I mean I know—I'll just be going now. If that's okay.

Tracy dashes for the exit. MacDuff moves to follow.

Hank: MacDuff? Next time you bring a singer, make sure she has more qualifications than simply being your girlfriend okay?

MacDuff clicks his heels together in a mock German show of respect, then exits. Hank collapses on the couch. Edie is uncertain as to what she should be doing.

Hank: If I knew then what I know now, I would never have bought all those Django Reinhart records.

Hank sits, seemingly unaware of Edie's presence. Silence.

Edie: You said you wanted someone to look at the books?

After a moment Hank moves. He slowly turns to regard Edie.

Hank: I need an accountant and they send me a girl scout.

Edie: I am prepared, Mr. Jeeter. I am a certified public accountant. I received my accreditation—

Hank: When?

Edie: What?

Hank: When did you get your accreditation?

Edie: Last month. But I scored the top of my class. I know what I am doing.

Hank: Have you ever done an audit?

Edie: Yes. In theory. It was part of the exam.

Hank: I don't believe this.

Edie: Mr. Jeeter, you called the office this afternoon asking for someone to come tonight. Believe it or not, most firms could not send you a fully qualified CPA on such short notice. Most firms would have turned you down flat. But not Fletcher, Monahan and Moss. They responded to your need. They sent you the most qualified accountant available. They sent me.

Hank: You're late.

Edie: Couldn't find a parking space.

Hank: I'm surprised you didn't come on your bike.

Edie: Mr. Jeeter, I can assure you that you are not going to find another accountant tonight. I am fully qualified and ready to begin and I have a fine head for figures. Just let me prove myself.

Hank: *Randomly listing numbers.* What's five thousand three hundred and eighty seven multiplied by twelve thousand seven hundred and two?

Edie: I'll need paper.

Hank: Fine.

Edie: Can you repeat it?

Hank: *Pause as Hank realizes he doesn't remember the numbers either.* Okay. You'll have to do.

Edie: So what exactly do you want?

Hank: I want you to look at the books.

Edie: An audit?

Hank: I spent the last week working on them. I want you to make sure I didn't make any mistakes.

Edie: When do you want this done by?

Hank: Midnight.

Edie: Midnight tonight?

Hank: That's right.

Edie: But it's past eleven.

Hank: You were the one who couldn't find a parking space.

Edie: *Pause.* I better get down to work.

Hank: You can work in the office if you want.

Edie: This is fine. This way you'll be close by if I have any questions.

Hank: Fair enough.

Edie: Thank you.

Edie starts to set up her workspace. Hank heads for the door.

Hank: Now I've got an emergency in the men's room.

Edie looks up for a moment, puzzled by this remark. Hank heads to the bar to pick up a wrench. Amelia is returning to the bar at the same time. Damon remains absorbed in his marking.

Hank: Have you found Quirrely?

Amelia: I'm working on it.

Hank: Keep looking. I've got a men's room to fix. If we keep sending people over to the gas station, no one is going to stay for the next set.

Amelia: They'll stay for your music, Hank.

Hank: That's the nicest thing you ever said to me.

Amelia: Why does everything have to be perfect tonight, Hank?

Hank: Just keep your eyes peeled for Quirrely. And don't let him get away this time.

Amelia: Or else?

Hank: Or else you might as well not show up for work tomorrow. *Exits.*

Amelia: Oh God. He *is* going to fire me.

Moonlight: *Entering with dirty dishes.* Something wrong, Miss Blue?

Amelia: Have you found Quirrely yet?

Moonlight: I've been bussing tables.

Amelia: Good. We can't have any unhappy customers.

Moonlight: We always have unhappy customers.

Amelia: Everything has to be perfect tonight.

Moonlight: And why's that?

Amelia: Hell if I know.

Moonlight: *Shrugging.* "It's all Greek to me." *Starts to exit to kitchen, but pauses by Damon.* William Shakespeare.

Moonlight & Damon: *Sharing the knowledge.* Ahhh! *Moonlight exits.*

Amelia: I make one little mistake and he's ready to get rid of me.

Damon: Perhaps the dilemma is not nearly as disastrous as you might believe.

Amelia: What do you mean?

Damon: Perhaps you should look upon it as an opportunity to examine some other prospects.

Amelia: I don't need prospects. I need this job.

Damon: Amelia, there is a certain question that has been preying on my mind . . .

Amelia: What's gotten into him?

Damon: Who?

Amelia: Hank.

Damon: My question isn't about Hank.

Amelia: Good. He never used to worry so much about business. He wanted to concentrate on his music.

Damon: Admirable.

Amelia: Ever since the boiler blew, he's been getting his fingers into everything.

Damon: Amelia, my darling—

Amelia: Moonlight is being run off his feet. And now this. I don't . . . *Noticing the sulking Damon.* I'm sorry, Professor. Is there something you wanted to ask?

Damon: Yes—

Moonlight rushes in.

Moonlight: Miss Blue. Come quick. Quirrely's in the kitchen.

Amelia: Great!

Amelia and Moonlight rush out leaving Damon alone.

Damon: Well. I think the moment has passed.

Damon sullenly returns to his marking. Meanwhile, MacDuff follows Tracy as she flees into the alley.

Tracy: I'm sorry. I really tried. I got all flustered. I couldn't think straight. I wasn't ready. He kept staring at me. And when he said that "Stardust" was a bad song—

MacDuff: He said it was a tough song.

Tracy: I just couldn't think straight. I knew he wouldn't like it. There was nothing I could do.

MacDuff: We'll just make sure you have another shot at it. That's all. Sometime when Hank isn't so busy and you're not so nervous.

Tracy: I'm going to be nervous. I know I'm going to be nervous.

MacDuff: You never get nervous singing around me.

Tracy: It's different with you. I know you. Singing around strangers, just makes me so . . . I'm sorry. I know you really wanted this.

MacDuff: Didn't you?

Tracy: I don't know. Maybe. I'm sorry. I can't think straight.

MacDuff: Relax. Don't think. It doesn't suit you.

Tracy slaps MacDuff at the insult. He laughs playfully. Back in the green room, Hank plunks the faulty faucet down on the dressing table and takes out his tool box. He starts taking it apart. Edie looks up from her work.

Edie: What's that?

Hank: Broken faucet. Nearly broke my wrist getting it off.

Edie: Why bring it in here?

Hank: The light's better. You know why I became a musician? To play music. So why am I fixing faulty faucets?

Edie: I don't know. Why?

There is a knock.

Amelia: *Popping her head in.* Hank? I have news about Quirrely.

Hank: You found him?

Amelia: He was in the kitchen.

Hank: Was?

Amelia: He got into an argument with the cook about the virtues of the vegetarian lifestyle.

Hank: And what did Raymond say?

Amelia: Something about three square meals, a balanced diet, and a lecture on how the meat industry supports the national economy.

Edie: That's true.

Hank: Oh God.

Amelia: By the time I got there, Raymond had thrown him out.

Hank: This keeps getting better and better.

Amelia: This guy's a nut, Hank.

Hank: An important nut.

Amelia: Why?

Hank: You just sell the booze. I'll take care of the high finance.

Amelia: Whatever you say. *Starts to leave.*

Hank: We're short of place settings.

Amelia starts to respond sharply when Edie signals her, encouraging Amelia to make a positive supportive response.

Amelia: I'll take care of it.

Hank: No. Give it to Raymond.

Amelia: I can fold napkins at the bar.

Hank: And is it my imagination or is it hot in here?

Amelia: I'll check on the boiler.

Hank: Thanks, Bluey.

Amelia: No problem.

As Amelia exits, Edie catches her eye and gives her a thumbs up.

Hank: She seems to be volunteering for a lot of work tonight.

Edie: Pretty indispensable.

Hank: She's got too much free time on her hands.

Amelia arrives back at the bar.

Amelia: *To Damon.* He's not going to fire me.

In the green room. There is a knock at the door. Moonlight enters with broom.

Moonlight: Just coming to do a little clean-up.

Hank: You can start right here.

Moonlight: *Sweeping.* You're fixing the faucets?

Hank: What do you mean *faucets*?

Moonlight: The other faucet just got broke. I think someone was trying to get the water going. Didn't Miss Blue tell you?

Hank moans in frustration and puts his head on the table.

Edie: Mr. Jeeter? I think you're lucky.

Hank: I don't feel lucky.

Edie: I wish I knew how to play a musical instrument. But the closest I'll ever come is this adding machine. If I could play, I think I'd play every chance I could.

Hank: How often do you play with that adding machine?

Edie: I don't play with it. It's my work.

Hank: Same with me. Playing is my work.

Edie: Oh. So you never *just* play.

Hank: I can't afford to.

Moonlight: If you don't mind my saying so . . . *Hank and Edie swivel in Moonlight's direction.* I'd say you can't afford not to play. *Pause.* It's not a matter of a guy wanting to play. It's a matter of a guy needing to play. A jazzman's music is the way he expresses himself and if he doesn't play, then it all gets clogged up inside like . . . like a busted water tap. Anyway, that's the way I've always heard it. Sorry for interrupting.

Moonlight exits. After a moment, Edie settles into work. Hank stares at the faucet and then his gaze shifts to his guitar. After a moment's thought he picks it up. He starts to play a tune.

Outside the green room door, Moonlight hears the music and smiles. He crosses past the bar as the tune follows. As he passes the bar focus passes to Damon reading from an essay as Amelia folds napkins and the music continues to play under.

Damon: She walks in beauty, like the night
        Of cloudless climes and starry skies;
        And all that's best of dark and bright
            Meet in her aspect—"

Amelia: Aspect?

Damon: Face.
        "Meet in her aspect and her eyes:
        Thus mellow'd to that tender light
        Which heaven to gaudy day denies."

Amelia: That's nice.

Damon: That's Byron.

Amelia: It's not everyone who is brave enough to talk about love like that.

Damon: That's true. Very true. Amelia. What is it you love?

Amelia: I love this club.

Damon: Ah. The club.

Amelia: Where else can you get good poetry and great music all in one place?

Damon: There are some who would offer the opinion that it was the poetry that was great and the music that was merely good.

Amelia: It isn't the ingredients. It's all in the final mix.

Damon: Very true. Very wise.

Amelia: Read on.

Damon: My pleasure.
"One shade the more, one ray the less,
   Had half impair'd the nameless grace
Which waves in every raven tress,
   Or softly lightens o'er her face—"

Amelia: Aspect.

Damon: Yes.

They share a smile as we crossfade to the alley. MacDuff holds Tracy.

Tracy: It's so strange.

MacDuff: What?

Tracy: In all these years we've known each other you've hardly said two words to me. And then all of a sudden we fall in love.

MacDuff: It just happens.

Tracy: This has been the best month of my life. When did you know? I knew I loved you that night you took me to the park and we sat under the stars. And you held me and . . . When did you know? When did you know it was love?

MacDuff: That's easy, Baby. The moment I heard you sing. I was walking to work and you were waiting at the bus stop and you were singing to yourself. You were just there, all by yourself and you were singing "Moonglow." It was like an angel had dropped down from heaven and decided to sing on the street corner.

Tracy: I didn't know you were watching.

MacDuff: The moment I heard you sing, that's when I knew.

Tracy: Oh, MacDuff.

Long, sweet kiss.

MacDuff: Beautiful.

Tracy: It's nice out here.

MacDuff: That too. *Pause.* I have to set up another audition for you.

Tracy: No.

MacDuff: I'll talk to Hank. We can do it after the next set.

Tracy: Please. I can't . . .

MacDuff: But you're so good.

Tracy: Why is this so important to you?

MacDuff: You have a gift, Trace. You have to share it. You can't just hide it away. If you don't—

Tracy: Okay.

MacDuff: What?

Tracy: Okay. I'll try again. For you.

MacDuff: You won't regret this. I'll go talk to Hank— *Starting to exit.*

Tracy: Do you have to do it now?

MacDuff: Why shouldn't I?

Tracy: I thought maybe we could stay here. A little while longer. Look at the moon . . .

MacDuff: Sure. No problem.

The music continues to play. We crossfade across the stage once more. As Amelia reads one of the essays, Damon is folding the napkins.

Damon: "She was a Phantom of delight
When first she gleamed upon my sight;
A lovely Apparition, sent
To be a moment's ornament;
Her eyes as stars of Twilight fair;
Like Twilight's, too, her dusky hair . . ."

Amelia: This guy hasn't developed an argument for his subject. And there's a lot of grammerical mistakes.

Damon: Grammatical.

Amelia: That too. I'd give him a sixty-five.

Damon: Sixty-five it is then. *Writes the number on the essay, then passing Amelia another essay.* Here's another.

Amelia reads the essay as Damon continues folding.

Damon: "But all things else about her drawn
From May-time and the cheerful Dawn;
A dancing Shape, an Image gay,
To haunt, to startle, and way-lay."

Amelia: Now, I like this one.

Damon: Really?

As Damon looks over Amelia's shoulder we crossfade back into the green room where Hank's song slowly comes to an end. Edie is well into her work, but when he finishes, she leans back and smiles.

Edie: That was great.

Hank: It was nothing compared to Wes Montgomery or T-Bone Walker.

Edie: Who?

Hank: They are the greats. Me? I'm just a minor key.

Edie: I thought it was good.

Hank: Not good enough. *Pause.* If I was good enough then maybe I could have brought more customers. When I bought this place I thought I was being so smart. Owning a jazz club, that's just like buying insurance. You'll always have a place to play. But it's distracting. Two weeks ago I was playing the midnight set and I suddenly realized I wasn't thinking about the music, I was thinking about repainting the walls.

Edie: The only thing you should be thinking about is how to be as good as Fish-Bone Montgomery.

Hank: T-Bone Walker.

Edie: Sorry. You should hire someone to manage this place for you.

Hank: Can't afford one. Can't afford new lighting fixtures either. Or a new sound system or new windows.

Edie: I thought I saw new windows out back.

Hank: That doesn't mean I could afford them. That was two hundred fifty bucks that was needed for a loan payment. My creditor was very unhappy about that. He's threatened to take the club.

Edie: That seems rather extreme. If I were you, I'd deal with another bank.

Hank: Who said it was a bank?

Edie: Oh. Maybe you could get an extension?

Hank: These people don't give extensions, they give contusions.

The lights jump cut to the alley on the shout.

Mike: Hey, MacDuff!!

Tracy and MacDuff jump. Out of the shadows comes Little Mike Conroy. A huge man, impeccably dressed in a sharp overcoat and fedora. He works very hard at exuding an atmosphere of menace.

Mike: How's it shaking, kid?

MacDuff: Fine, Mr. Conroy.

Mike: Looking for Jeeter. He in tonight?

MacDuff: Yes.

Mike: Thanks. See you on the flipside.

Mike enters the club. MacDuff lets out a breath of air.

Tracy: Who's that?

MacDuff: No-one you want to know. He's Little Mike Conroy.

Tracy: He doesn't look that little to me.

MacDuff: Yeah, well, wait 'til you get a load of Big Mike.

During this conversation Little Mike enters the club. He knocks at the green room door just as Hank is about to return the faucet.

Mike: Jeeter. Hey, Jeeter.

Hank: Uh-oh.

Edie: What is it?

Hank: Remember that loan I told you about? It just came calling.

Hank opens the door. Little Mike glides in.

Mike: Hank Jeeter. Good to see you. Who have we here?

Hank: This is my new accountant.

Mike: Where did you dig her up? The Junior Chamber of Commerce?

Edie: I'll have you know I'm a fully certified—

Hank: She's looking over the books, Mike. She's very good at her job.

Edie: Damn right I am.

Mike: When was the last time we saw each other, Hank?

Hank: February.

Mike: Long time not to hear from you, Hank.

Hank: I know.

Mike: I cut you a sweetheart deal. Fifteen per cent interest. At those rates I should be giving the money away.

Hank: I appreciate the support.

Mike: And I would appreciate you making your payments.

Hank: I'll have the money, Mike—

Mike: Mr. Conroy. This is business now, Hank.

Hank: Mr. Conroy. You have nothing to worry about.

Mike: I just walked through the club. Pretty empty for a Saturday.

Hank: It's been slow.

Mike: Jazz ain't what it used to be. It's all rock and roll now. Makes me wonder who's taking up all the parking spots.

Hank: Mr. Conroy, I'm selling the club.

Mike: And this is good news for me?

Hank: I'll have the money tonight. I've got a buyer all lined up. He's dropping by after midnight.

Mike: Midnight? Strange time for a business meeting.

Hank: He's a strange man. His name is Buddy Quirrely.

Edie: The bebop Buddhist?

Mike and Hank look over at Edie. Mike clears his throat.

Hank: Miss Moss, do you mind leaving us alone for a moment?

Edie: I suppose.

Hank: Take the books. You can work outside.

Edie: Um, sure. If I have any questions—

Hank: Write them down. I'll look at them once we're done.

Edie: If you think that's for the best.

Hank: I do. I really do.

Hank hustles Edie out of the room under Mike's watchful eye. Back at the bar, Amelia returns from delivering drink orders. Damon watches closely.

Amelia: You don't suppose Hank is in trouble with the IRS do you?

Damon: Hebe?

Amelia: Yeah?

Damon: We are fortunate enough to live a universe of infinite possibility and to live in a time that has provided us with a rich history and a far richer literary legacy. There are scientific discoveries made every day, and in every way mankind is evolving into a paragon of mortal species. This is an age of miracles, wonders, and excitement.

Amelia: Yeah?

Damon: So with all these marvels surrounding us, why on earth are we spending so much time talking about Hank Jeeter?

Amelia: I'm sorry, Professor. He's just . . .

Damon: Makes me wonder why you've put up with him so long.

Amelia: His music. *Dreamy.* When he plays he drives me crazy.

Damon: And when he doesn't play?

Amelia: *Angry.* He drives me crazy.

Damon: Sounds to me you're destined to go crazy.

Amelia: "I'm mad. You're mad. We're all mad."

Damon: Cheshire Cat.

Amelia: If only he'd stick to his music and let me do my job.

Damon: Then perhaps a more appropriate quotation would be "Off with his head."

Amelia: Queen of Hearts?

Damon: *Gazing at Amelia.* Queen of Hearts indeed. *Pause.* Hebe. Might I propose . . . a toast?

Amelia: You know the rules. The bartender never drinks on duty.

Damon: What's he going to do? Fire you?

Amelia: *Pause.* Just this once. For you.

Damon: This is a special night.

Amelia: And what are we drinking to?

Buddy wanders up to the bar just out of Amelia and Damon's sight.

Damon: Let me see if I can come up with something poetic.

Buddy: I need a decongestant.

Amelia: Perhaps to . . .

Damon: *Raising glass.* To subtext.

Amelia: Subtext?

Damon: Why not?

Buddy: Would there be a pharmacy nearby?

Amelia: *Focused on Damon.* All-night pharmacy just around the corner. Can't miss it.

Buddy: Thanks.

Quirrely exits as the tumblers clink.

Damon: Then here's to thinking one thing—

Amelia: But saying another.

Amelia and Damon drink. The glasses hit the bar. They smile at each other. And then with one thought ...

Amelia & Damon: Quirrely!

Damon and Amelia rush out in pursuit. Focus back in the green room where Mike and Hank are talking.

Mike: So what's the story on this Quirrely character? Why is he called the bebop Buddhist?

Hank: Buddy Quirrely used to work for a number of jazz musicians. Booked all the big acts. Made a fortune.

Mike: So he's an agent. I don't trust agents.

Hank: Then he had a revelation.

Mike: I don't trust revelations either.

Hank: Buddy claims he had a vision from on high, others say he got hit on the head real hard. You've heard of the Dalai Lama?

Mike: Sort of like a moose, right?

Hank: Yeah ... The Dalai Lama is the spiritual leader of Tibet. His followers believe that he possesses a soul so great that once he dies the soul is immediately reincarnated.

Mike: What does this have to do with jazz?

Hank: Quirrely's revelation was that if one great soul could be reincarnated, why not another?

Mike: So?

Hank: So, Buddy Quirrely has spent the last five years looking for the soul of Charlie "Yardbird" Parker.

Mike: You're not putting me on, are you?

Hank: He's coming over tonight. You'll have the money in the morning.

Mike: This is what I like to hear. You don't know how many favours I've done that have gone sour on me. And then things just get tragic. Terribly, terribly tragic. Imagine my relief.

Hank: And mine.

Mike: Although I could always just take the club. Call it even.

Hank: You're not getting the club, Mr. Conroy. Quirrely may be a nut, but he's a jazz nut. If I sell to him I know I'll have a place to play.

Mike: Get with the times, Hank. Rock and roll is where the action is. You should get out while the getting is good.

Hank: I won't give up the club.

Mike: Then you shouldn't have used it as collateral, Hank.

Hank: I'll get you the money.

Mike: Never doubted it for a minute. I know I can count on you.

Hank: I try, Mr. Conroy.

Mike: We're through talking business. It's Mike.

Hank: Mike.

Mike: I'll be back in the morning. And one more thing. Get that "Out of Order" sign off the men's room. Nothing queers a deal faster than bad plumbing.

Hank: Damn.

Hank exits with the faucet leaving Mike in the green room. MacDuff enters, but as soon as he sees who is in the room he turns to exit.

Mike: Hey, MacDuff. Where you going in such a hurry?

MacDuff: *Trapped.* Mr. Conroy. Sorry. I was just looking for Hank.

Mike: He's not going anywhere. You can talk to me for a minute, can't you?

MacDuff: Sure. I suppose. It's just that I'm not sure what we have to talk about.

Mike: Oh, I think you do.

MacDuff: No, really. We don't have to talk about it.

Mike: People who bet on horses shouldn't borrow money to pay off their debts. That's just trading one set of troubles for another.

MacDuff: I know.

Mike: And now your troubles are my troubles.

MacDuff: Don't worry. I've got everything under control.

Mike: That's what you told me last month. I haven't seen anything to convince me. My patience is running short.

MacDuff: Mr. Conroy—

Mike: I don't see how you're going to get the money, MacDuff. This place is dying.

MacDuff: Mr. Conroy—

Mike: If Jeeter were smart, he'd give up this whole jazz thing. Make this into a rock and roll joint.

MacDuff: Mr. Conroy—

Mike: Kids are where the money is. The only one I know who listens to jazz is my mother.

MacDuff: Mr.—

Mike: You have something to tell me, MacDuff?

MacDuff: The money's coming, Mr. Conroy. My girlfriend will be singing here.

Mike: So?

MacDuff: Between our two salaries, you'll have your money right away. I swear.

Mike: I didn't know you had a girlfriend, MacDuff.

MacDuff: It's all happened pretty fast.

Mike: And she's going to help you pay off your debt?

MacDuff: Yes.

Mike: Awfully convenient, MacDuff.

MacDuff: Mr. Conroy—

Mike: I don't care how you get your money, as long as you're getting it. But I'm going to keep my eye on you. You're a little slippier than I thought.

Mike exits. MacDuff collapses on the couch, releasing tension. Hank enters with the second faucet. MacDuff is immediately on his feet.

MacDuff: Hank.

Hank: Do you have a washer?

MacDuff: What? No.

Hank: Maybe I can make one.

Amelia abruptly enters.

Amelia & MacDuff: Hank, we have to talk.

MacDuff: It's about Tracy.

Amelia & MacDuff: It's important.

Amelia: It can't wait.

MacDuff: Hank?

MacDuff and Amelia look at each other.

MacDuff & Amelia: Do you mind? I'm trying to . . . I have to . . . I . . . Hank!

ACT ONE   45

Hank is feeling a severe migraine coming on. He puts his head in his hands to compose himself.

Hank: *To Amelia.* Do you have Quirrely?

Amelia: No.

Hank: *To MacDuff.* Is this going to take long?

MacDuff: No.

Hank: *Pointing to MacDuff.* You stay. *Pointing to Amelia.* You go.

Amelia: But—

Hank: We'll talk when you find him. Go.

Amelia angrily exits.

MacDuff: *As she passes MacDuff.* See ya, Babe.

Hank: *Tired, to MacDuff.* So, what is it now?

We follow Amelia as she returns to the bar. Damon is in his usual spot.

Damon: Are you okay?

Amelia: He's going to fire me. All he cares about is Quirrely. The guy has vanished and looks like it could cost me my job.

Damon: That is patently unfair. But perhaps I have something here that might cheer you up.

As Damon takes out the little box, Moonlight wearily enters, collapsing in a chair.

Amelia: Moonlight. How goes the nut hunt?

Damon returns the box to his pocket.

Moonlight: I've gone through every room in the building, combed the basement, and I sent the dishwasher out to walk around the block. We haven't caught a whiff of him yet.

Amelia: This is ridiculous. There aren't that many places to hide.

Moonlight: Could be he went somewhere else?

Amelia: The guy at the pharmacy said Quirrely was headed back here.

Moonlight: Maybe he doesn't want to get found.

Damon: Maybe he's on another plane of existence.

Amelia: He wouldn't leave without talking to Hank. Would he?

Damon: Perhaps we are approaching this matter from entirely the wrong angle. We know he isn't hiding. If we want to find Quirrely, then maybe we should try thinking like Quirrely.

Amelia: It takes a nut to catch a nut.

Damon: We know Mr. Quirrely's primary obsession. Left to himself he would undoubtedly return to his quest for the Great Soul.

Moonlight: Seems logical.

Damon: So where would you go if you were looking for "Bird"?

They think. Then the same thought occurs to Amelia and Moonlight at exactly the same time.

Moonlight & Amelia: The roof!

Moonlight: It's got to be.

Amelia: The fire escape has been down in the alley.

Moonlight: I've the key for the stairwell.

Amelia: You stay here and watch the bar. I'm going after Quirrely.

Moonlight: But . . .

Amelia: *Taking the keys from Moonlight.* I told Hank I'd take care of it.

Amelia exits. Back at the green room Hank is exiting with the repaired faucets. MacDuff closely follows.

Hank: Now which is the right one and which is the left one?

MacDuff: Come on, Hank. One more chance.

Hank: She had her chance. And unless she knows how to turn on the water, I don't need to see her again.

MacDuff: Please, Hank. This is very important to me.

Hank: Enough, MacDuff. I still have to check on the fire escape. I'll see you in ten for the next set.

Hank exits in a rush. MacDuff sullenly collapses on the couch again. But he becomes interested when Edie reenters and sets up her workspace. Glancing about to make sure there is no sign of Tracy, MacDuff moves nearby. Edie remains oblivious.

MacDuff: Hi there.

Edie: Pardon me?

MacDuff: Mickey MacDuff. I'm with the band.

Edie: Good for you.

MacDuff: And you are?

Edie: Edith Moss. I'm in the middle of something right now.

MacDuff: You look like you're working pretty hard.

Edie: I am.

MacDuff: This is a jazz club. You should be relaxing, not working.

Edie: Didn't I see you with someone earlier?

MacDuff: You mean what's her face? That's just a friend of mine. She was nervous about her audition and she wanted someone to hold her hand, that's all.

Edie: Listen. I really don't have time—

MacDuff: I can see you're busy. I just thought you might have time to chat.

Edie: I don't.

MacDuff: I know how it is. I have a set coming up myself. I play bass. But if you don't take time to relax, you burn yourself out. I understand. You have to concentrate. I won't interrupt. I won't say a word.

Edie: Thank you.

Edie returns to the books with renewed vigour. MacDuff pointedly leaves her alone. There is a long pause.

MacDuff: Is your father a thief?

Edie: No!

MacDuff: *A pick-up line.* Then who stole the stars and put them in your eyes?

Back in the alley Tracy sings "Moonglow" to herself. It is lovely. As she sings the back door opens. Unseen by Tracy, Hank listens to the song from the threshold. When she has finished he enters.

Hank: Hi.

Tracy: *Startled.* Hi.

Hank: What are you doing in the alley?

Tracy: Waiting for MacDuff. He told me to wait. And you?

Hank: I have to secure the fire escape.

Tracy: The fire escape? You mean that big ladder thing?

Hank: Yes. It has to be raised and secured.

Tracy: I think I did that already.

Hank: You did?

Tracy: Some guy went up there. It didn't look safe. I probably shouldn't have touched it.

Hank: No, no. That's fine. First thing that's gone right tonight as a matter of fact. *Beat.* Thank you.

Tracy: You're welcome.

Hank leans back and for the first time this evening actually relaxes. Tracy hovers. Hank finally glances in her direction.

Hank: So. You want to be a jazz singer?

Tracy: *Nodding, then:* No.

Hank: Good answer.

Tracy: MacDuff thinks I have talent.

Hank: Listen. Come back in a month say. When you feel more confident. It'll be better. Believe me.

Tracy: If you think so.

Hank: It's not easy you know. Late nights, long hours, lousy pay. You'd be better off working in a department store or something.

Tracy: Oh. *Pause.* But still, it must be wonderful to play. I mean jazz is such wonderful music and you play it so wonderfully. It must all be . . .

Hank: Wonderful?

Tracy: Yes.

Hank: Maybe it was. In the beginning. The music was all about emotions and sensations and feelings. I never thought about it, because jazz was always there. Right at my fingertips. But now . . . Too much to think about these days. I better head inside. I have another set in five minutes. I wish you the best, Miss Mason.

Tracy: Mr. Jeeter. I think you're really good.

Hank: I used to be better than good.

Tracy: Oh. sorry. I didn't mean . . . I mean I think you're . . . You're—

Hank exits. Tracy is off balance. Moonlight and Damon are at opposite ends of the bar.

Moonlight: His fingering is off.

Damon: He's overreacting.

Moonlight: There's something on his mind.

Damon: She wants to stay.

Moonlight: He's lost his sense of play.

Damon: She's had a hard life.

Moonlight: He loves his guitar.

Damon: Difficult childhood.

Moonlight: Played since he was young.

Damon: Never finished school.

Moonlight: Played side with all the best.

Damon: Working jobs without a rest.

Moonlight: Charlie Parker—

Damon: Valet parker—

Moonlight: Chet Baker—

Damon: Caretaker—

Moonlight: Brubek—

Damon: Coat check—

Moonlight: He even played with Mel Torme—

Damon: All the time looking for a place to stay.

Moonlight: Never more than just a side.

Damon: Then she found this place to hide.

Moonlight: Wanted a place that was his alone.

Damon: Claiming the bar as her very own.

Damon & Moonlight: It's where (s)he belongs.

The lights quickly catch Hank and Amelia passing.

Amelia: I've got Quirrely.

Hank: Great.

Amelia: He was on the roof.

Hank: The roof? Why not?

Amelia: Do you want to talk to him?

Hank: I've got a set. Make sure he stays put, keep him happy, get him a whiskey.

Amelia: He's drinking water.

Hank: Then get him water.

Amelia: He brought his own.

Hank: I'll see him after the set.

Amelia: So is everything perfect?

Hank: Close as we'll get. Thanks, Bluey.

Amelia: Just doing my job.

Hank: No, I mean it. Thanks.

Amelia: Hank. What's going on?

Hank: *Beat.* I better get out there.

Amelia: Break a leg, Boss.

In the green room, Edie is concentrating on the books, but MacDuff has not given up.

Hank: Come on, MacDuff. We're on. *Exits.*

MacDuff: *To Edie.* I'll see you later. *Exits.*

Amelia returns to the bar.

Amelia: Thank you, Moonlight.

Moonlight: You found him?

Amelia: Found him.

Moonlight: Congratulations.

Amelia: The set's going to start. Why don't you take a break?

Moonlight: Much appreciated. If you want me, I'll be out back.

Amelia: What do you do back there anyway?

Moonlight: Oh. Just pass the time. *Exits.*

Amelia: Why can't anyone give me a straight answer?

Damon: Perhaps it is simply a matter of asking the right question.

Amelia: And what exactly is the right question?

Damon: I thought you'd never ask . . .

The set starts. Hank and MacDuff are playing on stage. The music plays under the next scenes until the end of the Act.

Moonlight exits to the alley. Once there, he pulls a harmonica from his pocket. He smiles. He is about to play when he notices Tracy, still waiting.

Moonlight: Hello there.

Tracy: Hello. Aren't you supposed to be playing on stage?

Moonlight: I'm no musician, Miss. I just clean up. I like to come out here and entertain myself. The next set's just getting started. You might as well step inside.

Tracy: It's okay. I like it here. It's quiet. It's not so smoky. You can see the stars. On a night like this you can see so many of them. It's like they stretch on forever.

Moonlight: And how do they make you feel?

Tracy: Quiet. Peaceful. Small.

Moonlight: Nothing wrong with being small sometimes. *Tracy laughs.* Now, why are you laughing?

Tracy: If MacDuff were here he would be telling me that I was great. If my parents were here they'd tell me I was being silly. I think you're the first one who would just let me be small.

Moonlight: You look up at that sky and tell me what you see.

Tracy: Stars.

Moonlight: A lot?

Tracy: Yeah.

Moonlight: Well, you're not seeing all the stars. For every one of those you see there are dozens you can't.

We find Damon and Amelia at the bar. The dialogue shifts between the alley and the bar.

Damon: Amelia—

Moonlight: They're too dim—

Damon: My darling Hebe—

Moonlight: Or the city lights won't let them shine.

Damon: I have something I need to ask you.

Moonlight: But for all that—

Damon: A proposition if you will.

Moonlight: There's still a place for them.

Amelia: I'm listening.

Moonlight: If they were to go missing someone would know.

Damon: We have known each other for a long time—

Moonlight: Maybe one of those little stars is more important than the biggest star we see.

Damon: And I confess I have enjoyed every moment with you.

Moonlight: It might be a signal.

Damon: Rather let us say treasured them.

Moonlight: Or a home. It's the same with people. Some people may never change the world, never make the daily news—

Damon: Just a moment please.

Moonlight: Or even be remembered.

Damon: I need your attention.

Moonlight: But to someone—

Damon: This is very difficult.

Moonlight: Somewhere—

Amelia: Professor?

Moonlight: Somehow—

Damon: Amelia—

Moonlight: They make a difference.

Tracy: So what you're saying—

Damon: I was wondering—

Tracy: Is that there's nothing wrong with feeling small?

Amelia: Yes?

Tracy: Because everyone is actually important?

Damon: Would you marry me?

Moonlight: Yes.

Amelia: *Shock.* Oh my God.

Moonlight: At least that's the way it feels to me. *He points out a falling star with wonder. Tracy smiles.*

The music swells and fade out. End of Act One.

ACT TWO
A.M.

Nearly 1:00 A.M. The midnight set is nearly finished. A very pleased Damon is at the bar. Edie, taking a break, approaches.

Edie: Hello, Professor.

Damon: *Cheerful.* Edie! How spins the world of accountancy?

Edie: I'm almost done. I thought I'd order a club soda.

Damon: Hebe is engaged elsewhere. Allow me. *Slipping behind the bar.*

Edie: Are you allowed to do that?

Damon: Perhaps not under normal circumstances, but tonight is a night to celebrate.

Edie: Then you asked her?

Damon: *Pouring the drink.* The question has been appropriately popped.

Edie: And she said yes?

Damon: She asked for some time to think it over.

Edie: Oh.

Damon: Something the matter?

Edie: Well, it's just with that kind question you sort of hope for a big yes followed by hugs, kisses, and champagne toasts.

Damon: There is nothing wrong with taking time to think. It simply caught her by surprise.

Edie: Oh.

Damon: Something wrong with that?

Edie: No, nothing. It's just that if you're so in love with someone that you're willing to marry them, you sort of expect them to be thinking the same thing.

Damon: But we know each other. We've talked about poetry and life. We've talked about the world—

Edie: But never about yourselves?

Damon: It was implied.

Edie: Oh. *Pause.* But, you know, if I was getting married to someone—

Damon: Shouldn't you be getting back to work?

Edie: I better. *Beat.* It's just—

Damon: Good-bye.

Edie exits, leaving behind a suddenly concerned Damon. Over on the other side of the house, Hank rushes to the table where Buddy Quirrely sits. He appears to be in a trance. Amelia, who has been watching over Quirrely, shrugs.

Amelia: As soon as you started playing, he went out like a light.

Hank: Buddy? Buddy, can you hear me?

Amelia: I've tried that.

Hank: Have you pinched him?

Amelia: Didn't even flinch.

Hank: Smelling salts?

Amelia: I don't think he's breathing.

Hank: He has to be. Doesn't he?

Hank and Amelia closely study Buddy. He doesn't move.

Amelia: Nobody dies on my watch. *She leans close to Buddy's ear.* Hey, isn't that Charlie Parker?

Buddy: *Immediately alert and on his feet.* Bird?

Hank: Hey, Buddy. You okay?

Buddy: I thought I heard someone speak the Great One's name.

Amelia: Me.

Buddy: Have you seen the Bird?

Amelia: No.

Buddy: One should not take the Great Soul's name in vain.

Hank: We were a little worried about you.

Buddy: To achieve a greater appreciation for music I often put myself into a state of higher concentration. I noticed certain discordant patterns in your music tonight.

Hank: Nothing to worry about.

Buddy: Unshared troubles are a burden to yourself.

Amelia: And everyone else.

Buddy: A very true observation. Are you a Buddhist, my friend?

Amelia: I'm the bartender.

Hank: An occupational Buddhist.

Buddy: Shall we talk business?

Hank: Absolutely.

Hank pulls up a chair. So does Amelia.

Hank: Amelia. This is a business meeting. You should be back at the bar.

Amelia: What's going on, Hank?

Buddy: Who truly knows what is going on?

Amelia: Hank—

Hank: Amelia, please.

Amelia: I'm just trying to do my job.

Hank: Then get back to the bar.

Frustrated, Amelia exits.

Hank: I don't know what has gotten into her tonight.

Buddy: She has a right to know her future, my friend. You cannot protect a fragile blossom by keeping it in a cavern.

Hank: What's that? Some old Tibetan proverb?

Buddy: *With a quick smile.* "Better Homes and Gardens."

Hank: As soon as we're out of the woods, I'll let her know.

Buddy: I am hoping she will stay on if I purchase this establishment.

Hank: I couldn't run this place without her.

Buddy: And I am also hoping you will stay.

Hank: Give me a place to play and I'll be happy.

Buddy: This pleases me. Only the discovery of the reborn Bird would give me greater pleasure.

Hank: And how goes the quest?

Buddy: The Great Soul of Charlie Yardbird Parker, revered be his name, continues to elude me. I have searched the country, I have offered substantial rewards, all to little effect.

Hank: Just out of curiosity. When you find Charlie Parker—

Buddy: Revered be his name.

Hank: What do you plan on doing with him?

Buddy: Why it should be obvious. I will teach him to play the saxophone and then I will market him. Records, tours, talk shows.

Hank: There is a fortune to be made in reincarnation.

Buddy: I trust in the universe.

Hank: That's easy for you to say. You're rich.

Buddy: Yes. Yes, I am.

Edie enters with the books.

Edie: Well, I'm finished.

Hank: And?

Edie: The accounting practices are a little unorthodox, and there's one entry I can't quite figure out, but everything balances.

Buddy: I should like to see the books before I buy.

Edie passes Buddy the ledger. Hank and Edie watch with apprehension. Buddy opens the book to a random page, glances at the numbers and immediately closes the book once more.

Buddy: These are fine books. I approve.

Edie: That's it?

Buddy: I trust in the universe. If there was anything wrong, it would have been shown to me.

Hank: So you'll buy the club?

Buddy: Here is a cheque for many thousands of dollars.

Hank: Thank you. *Hank reaches for the cheque.*

Edie: But.

Buddy quickly pulls the cheque from Hank's grasp.

Hank: What?

Buddy: She said "but."

Hank: Why did you say "but"?

Edie: I don't think you should sell the club.

Hank: Why not?

Edie: This place could be a money-maker. All you need to do is divest yourself of some of your capital investments and streamline your operations. Within a year—

Hank: I don't have a year.

Edie: Just give me a chance.

Buddy: Let me see.

Buddy and Edie examine the books. Hank is desperately excluded.

Edie: Just look at the profit and loss statements.

Hank: Excuse me.

Buddy: You have so much invested in food?

Edie: Simplifying the menu frees up liquid capital.

Buddy: A slight raise in the cover charge—

Edie: Which is ridiculously low.

Buddy: —would be a simple way of insuring capital growth.

Hank: Buddy?

Edie: Then there is the potential of using the club as a road house.

Buddy: With relatively little risk to the proprietor.

Edie: It's all right there.

Hank: Excuse me, but I could really use that cheque right now.

Buddy: *Pause.* I trust the universe to show me what I need to see.

Hank: I know. You told me.

Buddy: And now the universe has shown me that I should not buy this club.

Hank: What?

Buddy: This place is your destiny.

Edie: You could be very successful here.

Buddy: Both financially and karmically.

Hank: I need the cheque.

Buddy: You think too much of the cheque. *Rips it in half.* I wish you luck in your club, my friend. And now I must go. *Standing.* The search ever beckons. Accountant girl, it has been a pleasure to meet you.

Edie: Thank you.

Buddy: Farewell, Hank Jeeter. Think of me. I shall know when you do.

Buddy exits. Edie brings the ledger to Hank.

Hank: You wrecked my deal.

Edie: You don't have to sell.

Hank: I need the money tonight. Quirrely was my last chance.

Edie: I was just trying to help.

Hank: I've got to find some way to keep Mike happy.

Edie: Mike?

Hank: By the way. You're fired.

Hank exits. Edie stands shocked at the table. Meanwhile Amelia arrives at the bar. Damon is waiting for her.

Amelia: He's going to fire me.

Damon: Are you avoiding me?

Amelia: No. Of course not. We'll find some time. Just the two of us. I promise you. *Beat.* Sorry, Professor. Have to run.

Damon: But I . . . *Amelia exits with a full tray. Damon is frustrated. He looks around for something to throw. Then he sees the pile of* *essays in front of him. With a vicious stab he marks the first paper on the pile.* Fail. *He starts going through the pile with an almost manic glee.* Fail. Fail. Fail. Fail! Fail! Fail!! Fail!! Fail!!! Fail!!! Fail!!! FAIL!!!! *He reaches the end of the pile with an almost postorgasmic exhaustion. He leans back in his chair.* Well. That was fun while it lasted.

A visibly agitated Hank enters.

Hank: *Stepping behind the bar.* I need a drink.

Damon: Something the matter? Perhaps I can help.

Hank: A little out of your ballpark, Professor.

Damon: I realize we have not had much opportunity to converse in the past, but let me assure you that there are some people who consider me quite insightful and informative. Some of them are even my students.

Hank: Hey, Professor. You like it here, don't you?

Damon: I would think that my constant presence would more than confirm the accuracy of your remark.

Hank: But you like it here, right?

Damon: Yes.

Hank: You would hate to see this place go, right?

Damon: I fear even to imagine such a nightmarish scenario.

Hank: How far would you be willing to go to save the Combo Club?

Damon: To the wall. To the brink. To the very gaping mouth of hell.

Hank: How would you like to buy the club?

Damon: Buy it?

Hank: I'm willing to let go cheap.

Damon: Buy the Combo Club?

Hank: I just need the cheque tonight.

Damon: *Laughs, then composes himself.* I'm sorry, Hank. I think you rather overestimate the value the community college places on my services. Although rich in the world of culture, I must admit a certain shortage in the world of finance.

Hank: Come on. You must have some money.

Damon: Have you ever seen my bar tab? It makes the *Encyclopedia Britannica* look positively emaciated.

Hank: Oh.

Damon: Hank, I am bound and determined to help you settle your dispute.

Hank: You know what's going on?

Damon: I should say so.

Hank: I haven't told anyone.

Damon: Amelia is in a constant state of distraction.

Hank: Amelia? Does everybody know?

Damon: You cannot keep secrets in the Combo Club.

Hank: I guess not.

Damon: You must take measures to remedy the situation.

Hank: But what can I do?

Damon: Talking might be a start.

Hank: This has gone beyond the talking stage.

Damon: There is nothing courtesy can't solve.

Hank: I could always lay low until the heat is off.

Damon: Put aside an afternoon and meet. Some place outside the club.

Hank: You mean neutral territory?

Damon: Exactly. Find some place cheery and relaxing. Maybe a sidewalk café. Or maybe the park.

Hank: A place with a lot of witnesses.

Damon: Talk honestly about your problems. You'll probably find it's all been blown out of proportion.

Hank: I don't know if that will work.

Damon: Then might I suggest a peace offering? Nothing so disarms an opponent as a little gift.

Hank: What kind of gift?

Damon: Perhaps a silk scarf. Something pretty.

Hank: Pretty.

Damon: And flowers are always nice.

Hank: Thanks for the advice, Professor.

Damon: I am more than happy to provide you with counsel. Nothing would make me happier than seeing the two of you kiss and make up.

Hank: Yeah. Right. *Exits.*

Crossfade to the alley, where MacDuff and Tracy are in the middle of a disagreement.

MacDuff: What do you mean you don't want a job?

Tracy: I just want to go home.

MacDuff: Now don't give up now, baby.

Tracy: Mr. Jeeter wants me to come back in a month.

MacDuff: We have to do this now.

Tracy: Why?

MacDuff: Maybe that first audition could have gone better. But you've got to get right back up on that horse.

Tracy: I don't like horses.

MacDuff: Okay—

Tracy: They're so big.

MacDuff: It's just a saying.

Tracy: And heavy.

MacDuff: Tracy—

Tracy: I used to have nightmares about *My Friend Flicka*—

MacDuff: *Snapping.* Shut up about the horses already! *Quickly composes himself.* Sugar. Let's go see Hank right now. Just the two of us.

Tracy: It's late. I'm going home.

MacDuff: Tracy—

Tracy: I think this is for the best. I really do. I'll see you in the morning.

Tracy exits. A frustrated MacDuff kicks one of the garbage cans.

Moonlight: *Entering.* Don't do that. I'm the guy that has to clean that up.

MacDuff: What do I care?

Moonlight: Listen, you may think you have troubles, but you don't get rid of them by causing other people trouble.

MacDuff: Boy, you're just a walking, talking fortune cookie aren't you?

Moonlight: MacDuff . . .

MacDuff: My troubles are my own business, man. The last thing I need is advice from some broken down old janitor. Who are you to tell people what to do? *Amelia enters and stands in the doorway, listening to MacDuff's rant.* The only thing you've ever succeeded at is cleaning up other people's messes. You're strictly minor league. And some time when you're old and feeble and still pushing broom, you're going to look back on this night and you're going to think how lucky you were to pick up Mickey MacDuff's garbage. *MacDuff exits. As he passes Amelia:* See ya, Babe.

Moonlight starts cleaning up, and is joined by Amelia.

Amelia: Are you okay?

Moonlight: Miss Blue? What are you doing here? *Amelia shrugs.* Some reason you don't want to go back to the bar, Miss Blue?

Amelia: No. No.

Moonlight: He finally popped the question, didn't he?

Amelia: How did you know?

Moonlight: It was pretty obvious to anyone with eyes.

Amelia: It wasn't obvious to me.

Moonlight: Have you decided what you're going to say?

Amelia: I like the Professor.

Moonlight: Good start.

Amelia: He's smart, he's funny . . .

Moonlight: But?

Amelia: What do you mean "but"?

Moonlight: Just sounded to me there might be a "but" coming up.

Amelia: There isn't.

Moonlight: Good. So what are you thinking?

Amelia: I think I should say yes.

Moonlight: Sounds to me you've got it all figured except for just one thing. I haven't heard you say the word.

Amelia: What word?

Moonlight: You know the word. The one this thing is really all about. Tell me Miss Blue. Between me and you. Do you love him? *Pause.* You know, I may not have had a lot of what some people would call success in this life. I've had a small kind of life and it's suited me. I've sort of set on the edge of things and watched the world pass by. But I've paid attention. I've learned a thing or two. Maybe nothing poetic and maybe nothing profound, but Miss Blue, one thing I've learned is you got to hold on to what you love.

Amelia: I love the club.

Moonlight: So do I. Anything else? *Pause.* Don't worry, it'll come. Don't think too much. Now maybe you should just get back to that bar.

Amelia: *Begins to exit. Pauses.* Moonlight? You're just a walking talking fortune cookie aren't you?

Moonlight: Am I?

Amelia: *Kissing him on the cheek.* Don't ever change.

Amelia exits. Moonlight smiles. He takes out his harmonica and begins to play. It underscores the next scene matching Edie's emotions.

Crossfade to the house. Edie follows a vaguely bored Foley. Edie has found the need to talk to someone and Foley is her unintended victim.

Edie: It's all right for you. You have a career. You're a piano player. The world's always going to need more piano players. But you don't know how fierce the competition is in accountancy. People think accountants are these mild-mannered, boring little rodents sitting in their offices tabulating figures and dozing between meetings. It's only a very few people who get to see the other side. The cutthroat, take no prisoners, dangerous side. Have you ever really thought about what an adventure it is being an accountant?

Foley: *Sitting at a table.* No.

Edie: *Joining Foley.* It's such a thrill, knowing that some innocent financial future depends on the sharpness of your mathematical skills and how quick you are with your pen. The pen *is* mightier than the sword. And you know why? Because the sword isn't tax deductible, but pens, now that's a legitimate business expense. Did you know that?

Foley: No.

Edie: Accountancy is a metaphor. A metaphor for imposing order on chaos. It's all about taming the unknown and then capturing it in neat little black and red figures. Can you imagine what this world would be like without accountants?

Foley: No.

Edie: I had such ambitions. And now look at me. Fired from my very first real job. I don't even have a resumé yet and it's already ruined. Maybe I get a little overenthusiastic. Maybe I talk a little too much. But is that any reason to get fired?

Foley: No?

Edie: But no regrets. If I had to do it all over again, I wouldn't change a thing. I showed him exactly how he could turn a profit. That's what accountancy is all about. Serving the best interests of your client. Damn it, I'm a CPA and no one is going to take that away from me! *Silence.* You're not really interested in accountancy are you?

Foley: No. *Exits.*

Edie: That's what I thought. But Miss Foley— *Follows her out.*

Crossfade to the alley where Moonlight is finishing his harmonica solo. Hank enters from the club. He absorbs Moonlight's music. He applauds at the end of the song.

Moonlight: Mr. Jeeter.

Hank: All these years we've been working under the same roof and I never heard you play.

Moonlight: Well, I may work under the same roof as you, but I play out here.

Hank: Maybe you could sit in one night.

Moonlight: I'm not that good.

Hank: Yes. You are.

Moonlight: Thank you.

Hank: We'll find some night for a jam session. Some time when there aren't so many things to deal with.

Moonlight: Something the matter, Mr. Jeeter?

Hank: Someone. I've got to see Little Mike Conroy in the morning.

Moonlight: What kind of business do you have with him?

Hank: You remember back in November? When the boiler blew?

Moonlight: How could I forget? No heat in the coldest week of the year. It got so cold we were using Foley's piano as a beer cooler. . . . Mr. Jeeter. You didn't.

Hank: We didn't have the money.

Moonlight: But Little Mike?

Hank: And now I can't pay him.

Moonlight: So what are you going to do?

Hank: I'll try to get an extension.

Moonlight: He'll break your legs.

Hank: I'm not letting him get the club.

Moonlight: You stay here. I'll be right back.

Hank: I don't plan on going anywhere.

Moonlight exits into the club. Crossfade to the bar. Amelia and Damon are each unwilling to be the first to speak. Silence.

Amelia: This is ridiculous.

Damon: Ludicrous.

Amelia: Crazy.

Damon: Nonsensical.

Amelia: We can talk.

Damon: Of course.

Silence. Amelia and Damon study each other. A depressed Edie enters and sits at the bar.

Edie: Club soda please.

Amelia: You're looking a little down.

Edie: I am.

Amelia: How about something a little stronger?

Edie: You're right. Tab. Large. No ice.

Amelia shrugs and serves the drink.

Amelia: Were the books that bad?

Edie: I got fired.

Amelia: You got fired?

Edie: I never saw it coming.

Amelia: I'm so sorry.

Moonlight enters at a run.

Moonlight: Miss Blue. You gotta come.

Amelia: What's wrong?

Moonlight: Mr. Jeeter needs to see you.

Amelia: Is it bad?

Moonlight: Oh yeah, it's bad. He's in the alley.

Amelia: *To Edie.* Looks like I'm next.

Amelia exits. Moonlight places himself behind the bar.

Moonlight: Hell of a night, isn't it?

Edie: Horrible.

Damon: Absolutely infernal.

Moonlight: *To himself.* Fun group.

Crossfade to the alley as Amelia enters to confront the waiting Hank.

Hank: What are you doing here?

Amelia: Moonlight sent me.

Hank: Thanks Moonlight.

Amelia: Hank, I know what's going on.

Hank: So I heard.

Amelia: You should have come right out and said something.

Hank: I didn't want to upset you.

Amelia: And when were you going to tell me?

Hank: I was hoping I wouldn't have to.

Amelia: You would have had to tell me sooner or later.

Hank: Not if I handled it right.

Amelia: So. I'm fired?

Hank: Fired?

Amelia: Hank, I need this job. And I think you need me too. I work very hard for you. And—

Hank: I'm not going to fire you.

Amelia: You're not?

Hank: You're the best bartender I've ever had.

Amelia: That's the nicest thing you've ever said to me. *Pause.* So, if you're not going to fire me, then what are we doing out here?

Hank: I took out a loan from Little Mike Conroy.

Amelia: You did what?

Hank: We needed money to replace the boiler. I used the club as collateral.

Amelia: You used the club as collateral?

Hank: What else was I supposed to use? My guitar? Everything was okay until you wrote that cheque for the windows.

Amelia: This is my fault?

Hank: I was just trying to save the club.

Amelia: Why didn't you talk to me about this?

Hank: I was taking care of it.

Amelia: Oh, you took care of it all right.

Hank: Well, I had to do something.

Amelia: Don't you know what this place means to everyone? To Moonlight? The Professor? To me?

Hank: I know, I know.

Amelia: We've got to talk to Little Mike.

Hank: I'll be seeing him in the morning.

Amelia: Then I'm coming too.

Hank: No. That just means four legs to break instead of two.

Amelia: He doesn't scare me.

Hank: He should.

Amelia: Well, he doesn't.

Hank: Well, he should.

Amelia: I'll take care of it.

Hank: Maybe firing you isn't such a bad idea.

Amelia: You can't fire me.

Hank: Can't I?

Amelia: Try it.

Hank: You're fired!

Amelia: Ha!

Hank: Scram!

Amelia: No.

Hank: Beat it.

Amelia: No.

Hank: Go!

Amelia: No!

Beat. Hank and Amelia throw themselves into a passionate kiss. It is broken as soon as they realize what they are doing. They stare at each other.

Amelia: *Pause.* The Professor isn't going to like this.

Crossfade to the house where a depressed Edie is gathering up her things. There she catches the wandering eye of MacDuff. With a smile he pulls up beside her.

MacDuff: Hi there. Remember me?

Edie: Oh yeah. You're with the band.

MacDuff: Finished your work?

Edie: Finished is exactly the word for it.

MacDuff: If you're not doing anything tonight, I get off work at about three.

Edie: What are we supposed to do at three o' clock in the morning?

MacDuff: I know this dive that's open all night.

Edie: Thanks, but I don't drink.

MacDuff: We can talk. I'm a very good talker.

Edie: I noticed.

MacDuff: It's not like you have to go into work tomorrow. Sunday is a day of rest. Why rest alone?

Edie: You've got to tell me. Has this approach actually worked on other women?

MacDuff: Come on. Give me a chance.

Back in the alley Hank and Amelia are standing at opposite ends trying to make sense of things.

Hank: I have a set coming up.

Amelia: Customers are waiting.

Hank: I have work to do.

Amelia: Me too.

Hank: Me too.

Silence. They remain frozen. Tracy enters, sees them locked in a gaze across the alley.

Tracy: Mr. Jeeter. Hello? *Pause.* Am I interrupting something?

Hank & Amelia: NO!

Tracy: I'm looking for MacDuff?

Hank & Amelia: Inside.

Tracy: Thank you.

Tracy exits into the club. Hank and Amelia remain frozen. Silence.

Amelia: What's going on here?

Hank: I don't know.

Amelia: Neither do I.

Hank: Maybe we should forget it ever happened.

Amelia: Good idea.

Hank: It was freak event.

Amelia: It never happened.

Hank: After all we have to work together.

Amelia: The club comes first.

Hank: I have my music.

Amelia: I can't be—

Hank: Oh to hell with it.

Hank throws himself into another kiss with Amelia. When they break they study each other again.

Hank: *With some satisfaction.* Okay. That one I planned.

Amelia: You did?

Hank: I did.

Amelia: Well, here's one I've been thinking about.

Amelia kisses Hank. While they are in the embrace, Mike enters.

Mike: Hello Hank.

Hank: *Freezing.* Is that who I think it is?

Amelia: Yes.

ACT TWO 77

Hank: Damn.

Cut to the house where MacDuff is leaning close in to Edie. He is whispering into her ear. Tracy enters just in time to see MacDuff kiss Edie. Edie immediately recoils.

Edie: What do you think you're doing?

MacDuff: Just relax, Baby.

Edie: God, this has gone on too long.

MacDuff: I can go for a very long time.

Edie & Tracy: What?

Tracy: MacDuff?

MacDuff: Tracy. What are you doing here?

Tracy: What are you doing?

MacDuff: We were just talking.

Edie: Oh geez. Don't tell me you like this guy.

Tracy: Yes. I . . .

Edie: I'm sorry. I didn't know. I thought . . . Wait a minute. Why am I apologizing?

Tracy: What were you doing?

MacDuff: I was just getting to know the accountant.

Edie: Edith.

MacDuff: Her. Because she was just feeling a little lonely. She was down and I was just cheering her up. Isn't that right?

Edie: No.

MacDuff: So, it's all perfectly innocent.

Tracy: MacDuff. She said "no."

MacDuff: She said "yes."

Edie: I said "no."

MacDuff: Listen, this is kind of a private matter.

Tracy: MacDuff? Is this what you do when we're not together?

MacDuff: *Beat.* Oh man, you're blowing this way out of proportion.

Edie: No, you're not.

MacDuff: Look, you're not really helping.

Edie: Are you sure?

MacDuff: Could you leave us alone?

Edie: I don't mind staying.

Tracy: MacDuff. What's going on?

Edie: Yes. You're such a good talker.

MacDuff grimaces in Edie's direction. Tracy waits. Cut to the alley where Little Mike is closing in on Hank.

Hank: Mike? What are doing here? You said you wouldn't be back until morning.

Mike: It's ten to two. That qualifies as morning in my book.

Hank: I don't have the money, Mike.

Mike: Then I've got some ideas on how to use this place.

Hank: You can't have it, Mike.

Mike: It's Mr. Conroy, Hank. This is strictly business now.

Hank: I won't let you take the club, Mike.

Mike: I'm going to get it either way, Hank. It's just that one way is easy and the other is tragic. Terribly, terribly tragic.

Amelia: You don't want the club, Mr. Conroy.

Mike: Will you tell your bartender to go inside so we can finish this?

Hank: Amelia . . .

Amelia: It's a bad investment.

Mike: I warned you what would happen.

Amelia: It's falling apart.

Mike: What are you talking about?

Amelia: Just going to cost you more money in the long run.

Mike: It is?

Amelia: There's tons of improvements that need to be done.

Mike: There are?

Amelia: This place is a dive.

Hank: No, it's not.

Amelia: Yes, it is. It's an old building.

Hank: There's still a few good years left in it.

Amelia: Who would want to run a business here anyway?

Hank: You love this place.

Amelia: It's a dump. You'd have to be an idiot to invest in this place.

Mike: Are you calling me an idiot?

Amelia: No!

Hank: Are you calling me an idiot?

Amelia: I'm beginning to wonder.

Hank: There are people who think this place could be a real money-maker.

Amelia: It's never going to be a money-maker.

Hank: We can streamline operations and within a year—

Mike: QUIET! Enough. I'm taking the club, Hank.

Hank: Over my dead body.

Mike: Good. We're back on track.

The alley door opens. Damon enters.

Damon: Hebe, my dear. I really need to know . . . *Everyone freezes as Damon takes in the scene.* Oh. Oh dear. *He senses danger.* Am I interrupting something?

Amelia: This is really not a good time, Professor.

Hank: No.

Mike: No, it isn't.

Amelia: We're just discussing a business loan.

Mike: A little privacy would be appreciated.

Damon: Then I should come back later?

Amelia: Yes.

Damon: With help?

Amelia: Help would be nice.

Damon: I'll come back then. *Exiting at a run.*

Cut to the house where Edie, Tracy and MacDuff are still at the table.

Edie: And then he asks me if I want to go out with him. At three o'clock in the morning.

Tracy: Three o'clock? What can you do at three o'clock in the morning?

MacDuff: Talk.

Tracy: What can you talk about at three o'clock in the morning?

Edie: Personally I think he had more on his mind than talking.

MacDuff: I was just keeping this poor chick company and she completely misunderstood everything. Look. I'm a bass player. You know how chicks dig bass players. I can't help it. They're attracted to me. It's the nature of the biz. But just because this girl is coming on to me, doesn't mean I'm untrue to you.

Edie: He is such a liar.

MacDuff: Who are you going to believe? Me or some lonely little skirt looking for attention?

Edie: What?

MacDuff: Come on, Trace. Just look at her. You know the type. Picking up men in bars.

Damon rushes in.

Damon: MacDuff. You have to come. Amelia's in trouble.

MacDuff: Not right now.

Damon: She and Hank are in the alley with Little Mike Conroy.

Edie: Little Mike?

MacDuff: I'm in the middle of something.

Damon: Something about a loan? You've got to come.

MacDuff: I don't care. They can take care of themselves.

Damon: I notifying the constabulary. *Exits.*

Edie is torn whether to stay or go; finally she runs after Damon.

Edie: Wait! What did you say about a loan? *Exits.*

MacDuff: She has a thing for me, Trace, and when I said I already had a girlfriend she went completely crackers. It happens all the time. Occupational hazard. You have absolutely no reason to be upset.

Tracy: I'm not upset.

MacDuff: Good. Neither am I.

Tracy: But I am disappointed.

MacDuff: Tracy—

Tracy: And hurt.

MacDuff: You don't have to feel—

Tracy: And humiliated.

MacDuff: It was her fault.

Tracy: And upset.

MacDuff: Tracy—

Tracy: I'm upset. Yes I am. I'm really, really upset.

MacDuff: Let me explain . . .

Back in the alley, Amelia and Hank are blocking the entrance to the club against the advances of Little Mike.

Hank: Let me take care of this.

Amelia: You're the one who got us into this mess.

Mike: Excuse me?

Hank: I did what I thought was best.

Amelia: Maybe I should do the thinking from now on.

Hank: And what's that supposed to mean?

Amelia: You're a great musician, Hank. But as a businessman . . .

Mike: Don't you guys ever shut up?

Hank: I—

Mike: Quiet.

Amelia: But—

Mike: Shut up. Thank you.

Edie enters through the door between Hank and Amelia.

Edie: Mr. Conroy!

Mike: Now what?

Edie: I have a business proposition for you.

Mike: Oh great. The kiddie accountant.

Hank: Edie, this is not a good time.

Edie: Mr. Conroy. I will have you know I am a certified public accountant. I graduated at the top of my class and received my professional accreditation. Here is my business card. *She passes him a card.*

Mike: *Studying the card.* I don't pay taxes.

Edie: Mr. Conroy, I want you to be fully aware of my credentials.

Mike: Why?

Edie: So you'll believe me when I say I don't write bad cheques.

Edie hands a cheque over to Mike.

Mike: What is this?

Edie: It's a personal cheque for two thousand dollars.

Hank: How did you—

Edie: It was the one entry in the books I couldn't quite figure out.

Amelia: Are you sure you want to do this?

Edie: Absolutely.

Mike: Now wait a minute—

Hank: We'll pay you back, I promise.

Edie: Oh, it isn't a loan.

Hank: It isn't?

Amelia: A gift?

Edie: An investment.

Hank & Amelia: An investment?

Edie: This place can be a money-maker.

Hank: I told you.

Edie: Under my management.

Amelia & Hank: Your management?

Edie: I'm the one who knows how to manage money.

Amelia: That cheque makes you a partner—

Hank: Not the manager.

Amelia: If anyone should be manager, it's me.

Hank & Edie: You?

Mike: Hey!

Amelia: I'm the one running the day-to-day.

Hank: She has a point.

Edie: Have you ever handled financial records?

Amelia: I can learn.

Edie: I already know.

Mike: Guys . . .

Hank: She has a point.

Amelia: But I know how to run the club.

Edie: She has a point too.

Mike: Excuse me . . .

Edie: So what are we talking about?

Hank: My department, your department.

Edie: I'll handle bills and finances—

Amelia: I'll handle the day-to-day.

Mike: Isn't anybody listening to me?

Hank: And what about me?

Mike: Hello?

Edie: You never write a cheque again.

Mike: Dangerous guy over here.

Amelia: Just concentrate on your music, Hank.

Edie: We'll handle the business.

Hank: Fine with me.

Amelia: Then we're agreed?

Edie: Agreed.

Mike: Sure. Why not?

Edie: Good.

Amelia: I want to talk to you about the cover charge.

Edie: Way too low.

Amelia: You think so too?

Edie: Positively. And we need to talk about food service.

Amelia: Too much, isn't it?

Edie: If we could divest some of the capital investments.

Amelia: The capital what whats?

Edie: Listen. I just want you to look at the books . . .

Amelia and Edie exit into the club. Hank is left with Mike in the alley.

Hank: Still want the club, Mike?

Mike: You guys are crazy.

Hank: Crazy is what jazz is all about.

Hank exits into the club leaving Mike behind. Back in the house, MacDuff and Tracy are still at the table.

MacDuff: *Patience finally cracked.* God, you're so pathetic. I tried. I really tried to help you. When I think of everything I've done for you.

Tracy: MacDuff?

MacDuff: You'd still be sitting at home listening to your stupid records. You're nothing without me. There are so many times I just wanted to shout at you, shake some sense into you.

Tracy: But—

MacDuff: I was the only person in this world willing to give you a chance. But you can't even do one simple audition for me. Anything at all you've accomplished was thanks to me. I'm the one you sang for. I was the one who made you happy. You can't do a single, solitary useful thing without me.

Hank: MacDuff!

Edie, Hank, and Amelia have entered and have been observing the last part of this rant.

MacDuff: Stay out of this, Hank. This is my business.

Hank: Whatever happens in this club is my business.

Amelia: And mine.

Edie: And mine.

Amelia: *Going to Tracy's side.* Are you okay?

Tracy: Yes. I think . . . I have to . . . Excuse me. *Exits.*

Hank: What were you doing there?

MacDuff: Nothing.

Amelia: You're just a selfcentred, petty little hustler aren't you MacDuff?

Edie: The word I'd use is jerk.

MacDuff: I just do what I have to.

Hank: And you're not a very good bass player.

MacDuff: Hey. I've just been trying to help that chick.

Edie: I've seen the way you help.

Hank: I will not have you mistreating people in my club. Especially not that singer.

MacDuff: She is no singer—

Tracy: Hello. *Tracy is on the stage. She is very nervous.* My name is Tracy Mason. I am . . . I am very pleased . . . *The microphone feeds back.* I am very . . . I would . . .

MacDuff: *Laughing.* Oh God.

Tracy: I'd like to try—I'd like to sing "Skylark."

Tracy starts to sing "Skylark" in a shaky, quavering voice.

MacDuff: *A heckle.* You're just proving my point.

It is going badly. Catcalls and heckles rise from the audience. Tracy is losing whatever nerve she had mustered. Hank leaps on to stage. Tracy is faltering and is about to flee, when Hank stops her by the shoulders.

Hank: Shhh. Just close your eyes and think about the song.

Hank has placed Tracy by the on-stage mike. She has her eyes closed. He picks up a guitar and starts to play "Skylark." With her eyes closed, Tracy starts to sing. She is almost as surprised as anyone else by how good it is. Her eyes open with startled discovery. She starts gaining confidence and as she does she starts to improve.

Moonlight enters. Hank spots him. With his head, Hank motions Moonlight on stage. Moonlight joins Hank and Tracy. The music steadily improves. It is terrific. When they finish, Edie and Amelia applaud enthusiastically. MacDuff sulks.

MacDuff: I don't believe it. Why couldn't she do that before?

Edie: Maybe someone was holding her back.

Amelia: Maybe she needed to sing for herself.

MacDuff: I knew that.

Amelia: What?

MacDuff: Why do you think I talked to her like that? She needed to be motivated.

Amelia: I don't believe this.

Edie: Believe it.

MacDuff: I had to get her up on stage somehow.

Hank: *Entering.* You're saying you were trying to help her?

MacDuff: Of course. I mean, Tracy's my girl right? I wouldn't do anything that wouldn't help her. *Tracy enters.* Isn't that right, Trace?

Tracy: You say you know what's right for me.

MacDuff: And I do.

Tracy: You say you want to help me.

MacDuff: I do.

Tracy: You say you love me.

MacDuff: You bet.

Tracy: You're a lying son of a bitch aren't you, MacDuff?

MacDuff: Tracy—

Tracy: No more, MacDuff. You used me. And you hurt me.

Hank: Miss Mason? I think you have some talent.

Tracy: I do?

Hank: With a little time and little confidence, I think you could be a singer.

MacDuff: That's just what I . . .

Hank, Tracy, Edie & Amelia: Shut up!

Hank: Tell you what. Why don't we get you a job here at the club? And you can sing when you feel like it.

Tracy: I don't know. It's all so . . . I . . . What kind of job?

Hank: *Turning to Amelia.* What kind of job?

Amelia: Well, we could use a waitress.

Edie: I don't know if . . .

Amelia: We'll find the money.

Tracy: There's just one thing.

Hank: Yes?

Tracy: You want me to sing?

Hank: When you want.

Tracy: It's just . . . *Indicating MacDuff.* I don't know if I could sing with him watching me.

Hank: Well that's no problem. MacDuff, you're fired.

Amelia: *To Edie.* I told you we'd find the money.

Edie: Fine with me.

MacDuff: You can't do that.

Amelia: We just did.

MacDuff: You can't fire me.

Hank: Get out, MacDuff.

MacDuff: You haven't heard the last of me.

Edie: Oh. I think we have.

MacDuff: Tracy . . .

Tracy: Goodbye, MacDuff.

A frustrated MacDuff exits. As he passes Amelia:

Amelia: See ya, Babe.

Tracy: You know that felt kind of good.

Edie: You made the right decision.

Tracy: I think so too.

Hank: Then everything is settled?

Damon: *Running in.* Good news. The police shall be arriving shortly. *Pause.* Something wrong?

Edie: *Pause.* I'll make the phone call.

In the alley, MacDuff angrily kicks a garbage can.

Mike: *Entering from the shadows.* You sure have a way of making messes for yourself, don't you MacDuff?

MacDuff: Mr. Conroy?

Mike: Not playing in the next set?

MacDuff: Sure I am. Just taking a little break that's all.

Mike: Don't lie to me kid. I've had a very bad night.

MacDuff: Mr. Conroy—

Mike: Let's talk a little business, MacDuff.

Mike pulls the whimpering MacDuff into the shadows. Crossfade to the bar where Damon finishes packing the essays.

Amelia: *Entering.* Some night, Professor.

Damon: As you say. But I am hoping that the night's disclosures have not yet been exhausted. *Placing the little box on the bar.* There is still one matter to be resolved.

Amelia: *Pause, then realization.* Oh, Professor. I'm sorry . . .

Damon: No need to apologize.

Amelia: It's just that so much has happened.

Damon: It slipped your mind.

Amelia: No. Not really.

Damon: *Beat.* I see.

Amelia: I have an answer.

Damon: I believe you have more than adequately answered the question.

Amelia: I didn't mean to . . .

Damon: No need to explain.

Amelia: I don't want to hurt you.

Damon: Of course not.

Hank: *Entering.* Do you have a minute? I think we should talk.

Amelia: Just the two of us?

Hank: I think we need some time together.

Amelia: Aren't I needed here?

Damon: No.

Amelia: Professor?

Damon: Go on. I'll be all right.

Amelia: Are you sure?

Damon: *Putting on his coat.* I am heading home myself. The marking is done. There's nothing more to stay for.

Damon starts to depart, Amelia rushes to cut him off.

Amelia: I'll see you tomorrow.

Damon: I'm not sure . . .

Amelia: I'd miss you.

Damon: *Pause.* I'll see you tomorrow then.

Amelia: "Entreating you not to forget your humble servant."

Amelia & Damon: *Identifying the quote together.* "Don Quixote."

Amelia smiles, then exits with Hank. Damon sadly watches her go.

Damon: "Though the night was made for loving,
    And the day returns too soon,
  Yet we'll go no more a-roving
    By the light of the moon."

As Damon has been reciting, Edie has entered also ready to go.

Edie: What is that? Shakespeare?

Damon: Byron, actually.

Edie: I don't know much about the Romantics.

Damon: Not many in this world do, I fear.
  "Tis all a Checkerboard of Nights and Days
  Where Destiny with Men for pieces plays:
  Hither and thither moves, and mates, and slays,"

Damon & Edie: "And one by one back in the closet lays."

Damon: Ah, my dear Thoth?

Edie: Thoth? What the heck is a Thoth?

Damon: In the Egyptian pantheon, Thoth was the celestial record keeper.

Edie: Kind of like an accountant to the gods.

Damon: Absolutely.

Edie: So how did it go with Amelia? Did she say yes?

Damon: She did. Unfortunately she said it to someone else.

Edie: Oh.

Damon: Tell me, Edie. Have you ever read *Cyrano de Bergerac*?

Damon and Edie exit. Music has been playing under the scene since the poem. In the starlit alley, Hank plays a tune. Amelia is lost in the idyll of Hank's company and music.

Amelia: You know what I think jazz is? It's living music for living people. It's about discovery.

Hank: About feeling.

Amelia: Healing.

Hank: Longing.

Amelia: Learning.

Hank: Loss.

Amelia: Poetry.

Hank: Music.

Amelia: Endings.

Hank: And beginnings.

Amelia: It's about love. Not the hot kind. The cool kind. The kind that won't burn itself out. The kind that lasts.

Hank and Amelia kiss. Light comes up on the bar. Moonlight is on duty while Tracy happily sits at the end.

Moonlight: It's minor key music for minor key people.

Tracy: Nothing wrong with that.

Black out.

DAVID BELKE was born in Winnipeg, but was raised, and continues to flourish in Edmonton, Alberta. He graduated from the University of Alberta with a B.Ed. and studied stage design there. He fills many different roles in the theatre: performer, producer, designer, award-winning writer, teacher. His plays have been presented across Canada—in Nanaimo, Saskatoon, Calgary, and the Victoria Shakespeare Festival among others—and in Northern Ireland, New York City, and Orlando, Florida. He has been writing a play annually for the Edmonton International Fringe Festival since 1990, and currently works as resident playwright and designer with Edmonton's Shadow Theatre. *The Minor Keys* is David's thirteenth play.

ALSO AVAILABLE IN THE PRAIRIE PLAY SERIES

The Aberhart Summer
Conni Massing
1-896300-40-5
$13.95 pb

Ethnicities: Plays from the New West
Edited by Anne Nothof
Contains: *House of Sacred Cows* by Padma Viswanathan; *Mom, Dad, I'm Living with a White Girl* by Marty Chan; *Elephant Wake* by Jonathan Christenson and Joey Tremblay
1-896300-03-0
$18.95 pb

Love and Human Remains / Unidentified Human Remains and the True Nature of Love
Brad Fraser
1-896300-04-9
$18.95 pb

The Hungry Spirit: Selected Plays and Prose
Elsie Park Gowan
0-920897-19-3
$14.95 pb

Rebels in Time: 3 Plays
Ken Mitchell
0-920897-05-3
$12.95 pb

NeWest Plays by Women
Edited by Diane Bessai and Don Kerr
0-920897-14-2
$12.95 pb